METHODS FOR EVALUATING HEALTH SERVICES

Volume 8
SAGE RESEARCH PROGRESS SERIES IN EVALUATION

SAGE RESEARCH PROGRESS SERIES IN EVALUATION

General Editor: SUSAN E. SALASIN, *National Institute of Mental Health*
Co-Editor (1980): LOIS-ELLIN DATTA, *National Institute of Education*

The Series Editors and the Publishers are grateful to those Board members who refereed this year's volumes.

SAGE RESEARCH PROGRESS SERIES IN EVALUATION
Volume 8

Edited by
PAUL M. WORTMAN

METHODS FOR EVALUATING HEALTH SERVICES

Published in cooperation with the
EVALUATION RESEARCH SOCIETY

SEP 2 2 1982

 SAGE PUBLICATIONS   Beverly Hills   London

For information address:

SAGE Publications, Inc.
275 South Beverly Drive
Beverly Hills, California 90212

SAGE Publications Ltd
28 Banner Street
London EC1Y 8QE, England

Printed in the United States of America

Library of Congress Cataloging in Publication Data

Main entry under title:

Methods for evaluating health services.

(Sage research progress series in evaluation; v. 8)
    Bibliography: p.
    1. Medical care—Evaluation.   I. Wortman, Paul M.   II. Series. [DNLM: 1. Health services research—Methods. W 84.1 M592]
RA399.A1M47   362.1'068   80-25069
ISBN 0-8039-1531-4
ISBN 0-8039-1532-2 (pbk.)

FIRST PRINTING

#6864164

CONTENTS

ABOUT THIS SERIES

The SAGE RESEARCH PROGRESS SERIES IN EVALUATION is a series of concisely edited works designed to present notable, previously unpublished writing on topics of current concern to the evaluation community. In keeping with a vision of evaluation as a methodological enterprise with outcomes at both the policy-making and services delivery levels, the series is designed to present state-of-the-art volumes for use by instructors and students of evaluation, researchers, practitioners, policy-makers, and program administrators.

Each volume (4 to 6 new titles will be published in each calendar year) focuses on themes which emerge from the previous year's annual meeting of the Evaluation Research Society—revised and supplemented by specially commissioned works.

The volumes for 1980 stem primarily from papers delivered at the 3rd Annual Meeting of the Evaluation Research Society held in Minneapolis, Minnesota on October 17-20, 1979. These volumes are:

UTILIZING EVALUATION: Concepts and Measurement Techniques, edited by James A. Ciarlo
EVALUATING VICTIM SERVICES, edited by Susan E. Salasin
METHODS FOR EVALUATING HEALTH SERVICES, edited by Paul M. Wortman
EDUCATING POLICYMAKERS FOR EVALUATION, edited by Franklin M. Zweig and Keith E. Marvin
Other volumes available in this series are:
QUALITATIVE AND QUANTITATIVE METHODS IN EVALUATION RESEARCH edited by Thomas D. Cook and Charles S. Reichardt
EVALUATOR INTERVENTIONS: Pros and Cons, edited by Robert Perloff
TRANSLATING EVALUATION INTO POLICY, edited by Robert F. Rich

THE EVALUATOR AND MANAGEMENT, edited by Herbert C. Schulberg and Jeanette M. Jerrell
EVALUATION IN LEGISLATION edited by Franklin M. Zweig

We are pleased that these volumes in the *SAGE RESEARCH PROGRESS SERIES IN EVALUATION* so well represent significant interdisciplinary contributions to the literature. Comments and suggestions from our readers will be welcomed.

Susan E. Salasin, National Institute of Mental Health
Lois-ellin Datta, National Institute of Education

1

Paul M. Wortman

University of Michigan

CONSENSUS DEVELOPMENT

Medical technology has become increasingly recognized as a major factor in our nation's health-care delivery system. In the past few years alone, there have been three major volumes on this topic published by the National Center for Health Services Research (1979a, 1979b) and OTA, the Office of Technology Assessment (1978). The focus of these reports has been the specification of methods for assessing the benefit-cost or benefit-risk of medical innovations. To a large extent this has consisted of the development and application of a conceptual framework for organizing the available information on a medical technology to facilitate its assessment.

In this introductory chapter we will describe and extend that framework, indicating its relevance for understanding and evaluating health services. The rapid diffusion of medical innovations

AUTHOR'S NOTE: As editor of this volume, I would like to thank a number of unsung heroines who have made it possible. Series Editor Lois-ellin Datta provided excellent guidance and arranged for informative editorial reviews that significantly improved the quality of the volume. My secretary, Jean Holther, handled the numerous thankless tasks involved in typing, revising, and coordinating with the authors—all with the highest dedication, excellence, and good humor. I and other chapter authors thank both of them. Finally, the author thanks Mr. Jack Langenbrunner for his assistance.

has, unfortunately, often resulted in instances of early success followed by later failure as more systematic information (often clinical trials) becomes available. Borrowing from statistics, we have called such innovations Type I technologies—those of little or limited value. In order to sort out the conflicting claims often surrounding medical innovations, NIH's Office for Medical Applications of Research (OMAR) instituted a novel evaluation procedure called "consensus development." Since 1977, NIH/OMAR has conducted a number of consensus development sessions (Consensus, 1979). The consensus development program represents a new approach to "technology transfer" undertaken by NIH. IT is derived from the pioneering work by Glaser (1980) and is a complex multivariable process that involves face-to-face meetings between groups of health-care professionals, consumers, and others to evaluate recent innovations in medical technology. Its purpose is to provide the "busy practicing physician" with an informed assessment of new medical technologies.

A MODEL OF CONSENSUS DEVELOPMENT

The consensus development process has been defined as the evaluation of "a specific medical technology for scientific soundness, safety, efficacy, appropriate conditions for use, and related factors" (RFP, 1980). Many of these terms have, in turn, been defined in the recent OTA report (1978) and are reproduced below. These constructs together comprise a conceptual framework or model for describing the technical consensus development (TCD) process (see Figure 1.1). We shall briefly define and describe these terms, noting their implications for measurement and evaluation. As we shall see, TCD is a meta-evaluation process involving a variety of evaluative methods that are discussed in the remaining chapters of this volume.

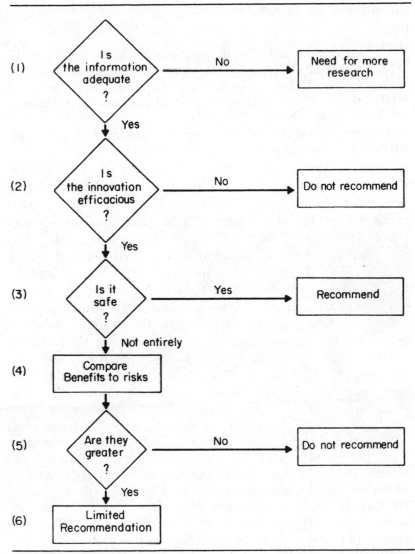

Figure 1.1 An Information-Processing Model of the Technical Consensus Development Decision Process

Adequacy of the Information

"Scientific soundness" is defined neither in the RFP nor the OTA report. In our opinion, however, it is a key concept for examining the TCD process. By "scientific soundness" we mean the adequacy and credibility of the information for reaching a technical consensus.

The first element (Step 1) in our model deals with the adequacy of the information. Is there sufficient data on which to base a judgment? While the inadequacies of any particular research study may be acknowledged, in many cases the newness of the technology is associated with a small and incomplete research base. This was apparent in the consensus development panel dealing with dental implants (Consensus, 1979: 13), where no agreement was reached on the advisability of mandibular staples. The panel was unwilling to base a recommendation "on the report of only a single investigator."

Other panels were similarly prevented from endorsing a technology by the absence of suitable data. For example, the panel examining breast cancer screening "deplored the lack of clear-cut data" on the benefits and risks of mammography for women under 50 (Consensus, 1979: 7), while the panel examining hemoccult screening for colorectal cancer did not endorse this procedure because of "insufficient data" (Consensus, 1979: 20). In the latter case, however, there were clinical trials under way that might eventually provide the necessary information. Thus, one problem continually confronting the consensus development panels has been the inadequacy of the available data on which to base a recommendation. This has led to a third outcome for many panels: Instead of "consensus" or "no consensus," they often call for more research. In fact, at least one panel—that dealing with the need for tonsillectomy and adenoidectomy—represented part of a continuing effort to develop a "prospective clinical trial" to assess the efficacy of these procedures (Consensus, 1979: 27).

The problems involved in generating adequate information are amply illustrated by Esrov (Chapter 2). She discusses the often neglected, but crucial, problems in the management and conduct of a health services evaluation. Esrov describes an ill-fated evaluation of a variety of physician peer review models. A major aspect of this project involved the collection of a large amount of hospital-based patient data so that judgments about quality of care could be made. The problems in data management eventually proved insuperable. Esrov offers some guidelines for personnel selection, training, supervision, and other data quality control procedures. These address factors that affect the quality and hence the adequacy of evaluative data.

Research Quality. Once the adequacy of the information has been determined, the credibility of the evidence must be examined. We define this aspect of scientific soundness to mean the internal validity[1] (Campbell and Stanley, 1966) or quality of the research methodology employed in producing evidence on the efficacy, safety, and appropriateness of a medical innovation. More specifically, it refers to the process of attributing causality for the observed effects of a new technology (Wortman, 1975). The premier research methodology is the "true" experiment or, in health services, the randomized, controlled, clinical trial (RCT). This methodology protects against a variety of competing alternative explanations or "plausible rival hypotheses."

Although some believe that other less costly and less time-consuming methods such as trials using historical controls (Gehan and Freireich, 1974) are acceptable, there is much dispute on this point (Byar et al., 1976). While other researchers (Gilbert et al., 1977: 686; Riecken et al., 1974: 112) have provided convincing evidence derived from nonrandomized studies, these are, in our opinion, the exception that proves the rule. More important, scientific soundness goes beyond the methodological quality of the individual research study. A thorough technology assessment must encompass all available information and examine the overall pattern of evidence that emerges. This view is based on two assumptions. The first is the widely held scientific belief in the replicability of important phenomena. The second is a less commonly held belief that no single study, even an RCT, is definitive.

Pattern of Evidence. The chapter by Wortman (Chapter 3) examines the role of RCTs in evaluating medical innovations. It graphically illustrates that the supporting evidence for Type I technologies often rests on weak, quasi-experimental research. When the total pattern of research evidence is displayed, it is all too likely to reveal early, but methodologically crude, support, followed later by strong, but nonsupportive, RCTs. Wortman discusses some of the factors contributing to the temporal lag in RCTs as well as other problems that limit their utility.

This approach involves a complete summary of all the available research evidence tabulated by outcome and methodology. Such a summary could be used to address the issues of both efficacy and safety. In fact, this analysis can inform not only the consensus development process, but also indicate problems it may encounter. For example, spurious consensus could arise when certain information is either ignored (perhaps due to participant selection) or unavailable (due to publication lags). Alternatively, lack of consensus could develop when participants have knowledge of different studies. In both of these cases the consensus development process would be flawed. The psychological literature has already demonstrated that it is difficult to synthesize a large body of information (i.e., so-called cognitive strain by Bruner et al., 1956) and that cognitive biases can lead to distortions in evaluating flawed studies (Nisbett and Ross, 1980).

Efficacy

The next element in our model (Step 2) deals with the efficacy of the technology. The discussion of scientific soundness has referred to efficacy in a number of places. Efficacy is a complex concept that includes a number of components. It has been defined as

the probability of benefit to individuals in a defined population from a medical technology applied for a given medical problem under ideal conditions of use [Office of Technology Assessment, 1978: 14].

The most important of the "factors" in the definition is the benefit(s) of the technology being evaluated. The determination of benefit involves a judgment of worth that is dependent on the evaluative criteria (e.g., mortality, morbidity, survival rates) that are used. The choice and interpretation of these criteria can dramatically affect the consensus process.

Criteria. Even where the participants have access to the same information, it is likely that they will not always agree on the criteria to be used in evaluating an innovation. The Office of Technology Assessment report (1978: 15) notes that there are five different criteria that can be examined to determine the benefit (which is one aspect of efficacy) of a diagnostic technology such as the CT scanner:

(1) *Technical capability:* Does the device perform reliably and deliver accurate information?
(2) *Diagnostic accuracy:* Does use of the device permit accurate diagnoses?
(3) *Diagnostic impact:* Does use of the device replace other diagnostic procedures, including surgical exploration and biopsy?
(4) *Therapeutic impact:* Do results obtained from the device affect planning and delivery of therapy?
(5) *Patient outcome:* Does use of the device contribute to improved health of the patient?

Assuming that the consensus panel focuses on the same criteria (as they have done in most cases), there still may be some disagreement in interpreting the evidence. For example, McNeil (1979) discusses a number of measures (such as sensitivity and specificity) for assessing "diagnostic accuracy" and indicates a problem in interpretation that can occur when they are not consistently better than those of an alternative (often the existing) technology. There are three problems here: emphasis on one of a number of measures, problems in combining multiple evaluative criteria, and assessing the significance of the results. Thus, one participant may weigh the false positive rate (1 - specificity) more heavily, while another stresses the true positive rate (sensitivity). This would lead to a lack of agreement, an extension of the discussion, and perhaps a lack of consensus. Even if there were agreement that the results should be reduced to one measure, they might not have that information or be able to derive the receiver operating characteristic

(ROC) curve that combines these two measures. Finally, once this was accomplished, they may not be able to agree on whether a better ROC curve indicates a significant improvement over the existing technology.

Yeaton and Sechrest (Chapter 4) discuss the problems in determining the size and significance of the outcomes or effects of health service interventions. They describe three "features of research" that can influence the magnitude of the observed outcomes. These features overlap and extend the components in OTA's definition of efficacy. The authors then describe a number of methods for determining effect sizes, including the use of experts, as is done in consensus development. They also discuss appropriate comparative standards for assessing health service innovations.

Problem. The three other factors involved in the definition of efficacy are: the medical problem, population, and conditions. All can influence the determination of efficacy. The appropriateness of the technology for the medical problem often is central to its assessment. In many innovations in health services, such as the CT scanner, appropriateness is difficult to determine. Such "system management technologies" (Rosenthal, 1979) have a broad, but often diffuse, impact on patient health status. Rogers, Haring, and Goetz (Chapter 5) describe the application of a novel evaluation technique called tracer methodology. This involves a targeted assessment of the innovation, usually by selecting a few diseases and tracing the impact of the health service on them. Rogers and his associates report on an RCT using this evaluative method to assess the impact of a medical information system on patient health.

Population. The population affected is also an important consideration in assessing efficacy. One of the major concerns is the generalizability or external validity of the findings to other patients. The recently concluded study of a "systematic antihypertensive program" for patients with high blood pressure provides an example of the successful extension (using an RCT) of an existing technology to a new (though related) medical problem (Hypertension Detection and Follow-Up Program Cooperative Group, 1979). In particular, the efficacy of the drug therapy for participants with mild hypertension was demonstrated "for the first time."

Conditions. Our discussion of efficacy underscores the need for credible evidence in assessing medical innovations, especially technologies that have become controversial. Generally, RCTs have played a major role in arbitrating these disputes, but only when these studies have been found to be efficacious. For example, Wortman (in Chapter 3) discusses some of the problems with a major RCT of coronary artery bypass surgery. The study was attacked for the poor "conditions of use." Thus, critics concluded that the RCT apparently was not performed under "ideal" circumstances. Other related conditions, such as the quality of the equipment, facilities, and support personnel, also can influence the outcome of the technology. The logic underlying the use of "ideal conditions" in assessing efficacy is to eliminate these factors as plausible rival hypotheses or alternative explanations for poor outcomes. Yeaton and Sechrest (Chapter 4) refer to this as "integrity of treatment."

Safety

If a technology is found to be of some benefit, then an examination of the risks involved in appropriate (Step 3). Obviously, if there are no apparent or significant benefits, then a discussion of safety is not necessary. Nevertheless, many consensus development panels have investigated both issues simultaneously, given the uncertainty of the evidence and the need to provide a comprehensive assessment in a short time (e.g., breast cancer screening and dental implants).

Safety and risk, as defined by OTA (1978: xii), mirror efficacy in the factors that must be considered:

Risk—A measure of the probability of an adverse or untoward outcome occurring and the severity of the resultant harm to health of individuals in a defined population associated with use of a medical technology applied for a given medical problem under specified conditions of use.

Safety—A judgment of the acceptability of relative *risk* in a specified situation.

From an information-processing perspective, then, the processes and issues raised above with respect to efficacy are applicable to safety as well. However, safety is often more difficult to assess than efficacy. The reason for this is the lack of relevant outcome information on the risks involved.

Risk. Technologies are developed and diffused with their potential benefits in mind. Thus, the evidence is often focused on benefits rather than risk. Moreover, it is frequently difficult to predict or assess risk until there is some extensive experience with the innovation. This presents not only a dilemma for the consensus development process, but also for those desiring the earliest possible assessment of medical innovations. The absence of data on radiation risk from mammography is but one example of the problems faced in this area. As a result, there may exist a general information bias toward underestimating the risks and hence the safety of a new medical technology.

The implications of inadequate information for a general decision on the benefit-risk ratio are obvious (Step 4). Even with a balanced, highly informed panel, an inappropriate consensus may be reached. If there is a lack of available information concerning safety, it may bias the judgment toward a positive assessment (Step 5). For this reason it is important that the broadest possible spectrum of persons (involved with the technology) participate in the consensus process. As Wagner (1979) notes in discussing the use of experts, they may take a "narrow view" of the risks and benefits posed by a technology.

Yeaton and Sechrest (Chapter 4) discuss some simple heuristics for assessing risk and making decisions on the benefits and costs or risks of a health intervention. Thompson and Cohen focus on this problem (Chapter 6). They describe a methodology for measuring uncertainty (i.e., risk) called decision analysis, and compare it with benefit-cost analysis. The methodology is illustrated by applying it to the current controversy surrounding electronic fetal monitoring.

Ethics

One essential perspective in the consensus development process is that of the patient or recipient of the technology. The consumers of a technology presumably would be less likely to underestimate the potential risks involved and thus counterbalance the professional viewpoint noted above. Moreover, the inclusion of a consumer's or patient's perspective is seen as meeting current ethical standards that have evolved from recent legal and governmental actions. Specifically, ethical concerns are reflected in legal requirements for informed consent (Faden and Faden, 1978) and federal regulations establishing institutional review boards (IRBs) to examine all requests for research funds involving human subjects (Gray et al., 1978).

Once the efficacy and safety of the medical innovation have been assessed and compared, an overall consensus consisting of a number of recommendations should result. In most cases, the panels have reached qualified endorsements of the technology (e.g., regular breast screening only for women over 50). Part of these limited recommendations (Step 6) have usually included requirements for improved informed-consent procedures. As noted above, this reflects a growing awareness of the real risks posed by new technologies and the rights of patients to participate in making health-related decisions. In many cases, lay groups and bioethicists have participated in the consensus development process (e.g., the Conference on Antenatal Diagnosis).

Policy Impact. The consensus development process has resulted in a number of important policy recommendations and changes that reflect ethical concerns. This is particularly evident for the panels dealing with breast cancer. The panel concerned with screening made a number of recommendations on limiting routine screening to women over 50. This was quickly translated into policy for the Breast Cancer Detection Demonstration Projects (Culliton, 1977). Moreover, they decided to notify all women who had mastectomies based on incorrect pathology reports (i.e., the tissue was found on reexamination to be nonmalignant). As a result, the panel recommended a two-step procedure in dealing with women found to have malignancies—a decision that was reaffirmed by the consensus development conference on "The Treatment of Primary Breast Cancer: Management of Local Disease" (New England Journal of Medicine, 1979).

This panel also recommended total mastectomy with axillary dissection as the standard treatment replacing the Halsted radical mastectomy. These recommendations allow women to choose surgery or some other treatment as well as the type of surgery. The results indicate the sensitivity of the process to the ethical issues surrounding patients' rights and the need for informed consent. Although some critics (e.g., Veatch, 1980) believe the values of the experts selected to such panels generally predispose them to a lack of concern with the patient's perspective, these and other consensus development activities indicate a growing cognizance of patients' rights.

CONCLUSION

The NIH consensus development program represents a novel evaluation procedure aimed at utilizing scientific information. Evaluators have been concerned about the direct application or utilization of their findings. The low incidence of such impact has resulted in a reconsideration of the meaning of this term (see Alkin et al., 1979; Weiss, 1977). These authors maintain that utilization is an indirect process, with the evaluation findings affecting the decision- and policy-makers' conception of an issue or problem. In its brief history, however, consensus development has already influenced a number of policy decisions. Does this imply that yet another redefinition of utilization is in order? Perhaps. We can only speculate on the reasons for this impact. Two—location and content—seem relevant. The consensus process is a formal mechanism conducted by a major governmental agency with a mandate to apply or transfer knowledge. As such, it is not confined to considering the worth or utility of a single evaluation, but the entire "pattern of evidence" derived from all studies of the technology. These factors may contribute to the instrumental utilization associated with the consensus program.

As we have seen, consensus development represents a significant evaluation procedure that depends on a number of specific methodologies. The remaining chapters in this volume describe some of the evaluation techniques that are useful in reaching an appropriate assessment of or informed consensus on innovations in health services.

NOTE

1. External validity is also important in technology assessment. This concept is considered as one aspect of efficacy, as is discussed in that section.

REFERENCES

ALKIN, M. C., R. DAILLAK, and P. WHITE (1979) Using Evaluations: Does Evaluation Make a Difference? Beverly Hills, CA: Sage.
BRUNER, J. S., J. J. GOODNOW, and G. A. AUSTIN (1956) A Study of Thinking. New York: John Wiley.
BYAR, D. P., R. M. SIMON, W. T. FRIEDEWALD, J. J. SCHLESSELMAN, D. L. DEMETS, J. H. ELLENBERG, M. H. GAIL, and J. H. WARE (1976) "Randomized clinical trials: Perspectives on some recent ideas." New England Journal of Medicine 295: 74-80.
CAMPBELL, D. T. and J. C. STANLEY (1966) Experimental and Quasi-experimental Designs for Research. Skokie, IL: Rand McNally.
Consensus (1979) National Institutes of Health Consensus Development Conference Summaries, Volume 1, 1977-1978. Bethesda, MD: National Institutes of Health.
CULLITON, B. J. (1977) "Cancer Institute unilaterally issues new restrictions on mammography." Science 196: 853-857.
FADEN, A. I. and R. R. FADEN (1978) "Informed consent in medical practice: with particular reference to neurology." Archives of Neurology 35: 761-764.
GEHAN, E. A. and E. J. FREIREICH (1974) "Non-randomized controls in cancer clinical trials." New England Journal of Medicine 290: 198-203.
GILBERT, J. P., B. McPEEK, and F. MOSTELLER (1977) "Statistics and ethics in surgery and anesthesia." Science 198: 684-689.
GLASER, E. M. (1980) "Using behavioral science strategies for defining the state-of-the-art." Journal of Applied Behavioral Science 16: 79-92.
GRAY, B. H., R. A. COOKE, and A. TANNENBAUM (1978) "Research involving human subjects." Science 201: 1094-1101.
Hypertension Detection and Follow-Up Program Cooperative Group (1979) "Five-year findings of the hypertension detection and follow-up program. I. Reduction in mortality of persons with high blood pressure, including mild hypertension." Journal of the American Medical Association 242: 2562-2571.
McNEIL, B. J. (1979) "Pitfalls in and requirements for diagnostic technologies," in Medical Technology. NCHSR Research Proceedings Series, DHEW Publication (PHS) 79-3254. Washington, DC: Government Printing Office.

National Center for Health Services Research (1979a) Medical Technology. NCHSR Research Proceedings Series, DHEW Publication (PHS) 79-3254. Washington, DC: Government Printing Office.

——— (1979b) Medical Technology: The Culprit Behind Health Care Costs? Proceeding of the 1977 Sun Valley Forum on National Health, DHEW Publication (PHS) 79-3216. Washington, DC: Government Printing Office.

New England Journal of Medicine (1979) "Treatment of primary breast cancer." 301: 340.

NISBETT, R. and L. ROSS (1980) Human Inference: Strategies and Shortcomings of Social Judgment. Englewood Cliffs, NJ: Prentice-Hall.

Office of Technology Assessment (1978) Assessing the Efficacy and Safety of Medical Technologies. Washington, DC: Government Printing Office.

RFP (1980) Evaluation of NIH Consensus Development Process Bethesda, MD: National Institutes of Health. (NIH-OD-80-18)

RIECKEN, H. W., R. F. BORUCH, D. T. CAMPBELL, N. CAPLAN, T. K. GLENNAN, J. W. PRATT, A. REES, and W. WILLIAMS (1974) Social Experimentation: A Method for Planning and Evaluating Social Intervention. New York: Academic.

ROSENTHAL, G. (1979) "Anticipating the costs and benefits of new technology: a typology for policy," in National Center for Health Services Research, Medical Technology: The Culprit Behind Health Care Costs? Proceedings of the 1977 Sun Valley Forum on National Health, DHEW Publication (PHS) 79-3216. Washington, DC: Government Printing Office.

VEATCH, R. M. (1980) "Voluntary risks to health: the ethical issues." Journal of the American Medical Association 243: 50-55.

WAGNER, J. L. (1979) "Toward a research agenda on medical technology," in Medical Technology. NCHSR Research Proceedings Series, DHEW Publication (PHS) 79-3254. Washington, DC: Government Printing Office.

WEISS, C. H. (1977) Using Social Research in Public Policy Making. Lexington, MA: D. C. Heath.

WORTMAN, P. M. (1975) "Evaluation research: a psychological perspective." American Psychologist 30: 562-575.

Linda V. Esrov

National Center for Health Services Research

2

ASSURING DATA QUALITY IN SERVICES EVALUATION

While evaluations of health services interventions include many of the same methodological problems found in other disciplines (see Gilbert et al., 1975; Sechrest and Cohen, 1979), they often involve substantial complexity in the area of data management. Although this problem may not be unique to such evaluations, the complexity of data-related tasks may be unfamiliar to those researchers who are otherwise knowledgeable about health services or the evaluation of health programs. As a result, inadequate planning to assure data quality may lead to severe data management problems. Even researchers who have considerable experience with complex clinical data may continue to be challenged by the inherent difficulties of the data management tasks.

This chapter describes a large-scale federal health services evaluation whose staff the author joined during the project. This evaluation had already developed some major data manage-

AUTHOR'S NOTE: This chapter is a revision of a paper presented at the Third Annual Meeting of the Evaluation Research Society in Minneapolis, Minnesota, October 18-20, 1979. The views expressed here are those of the author, and no official endorsement by the National Center for Health Services Research is intended or should be inferred.

ment problems, at least in part because there had never been adequate attention to assuring data quality. Eventually, the project's data problems proved to be quite resistant to remedial changes. The purpose of describing this project is to provide both background and context for developing guidelines for assuring data quality, especially in situations where the data source is the medical record. This discussion is intended to emphasize the pivotal role that data management can play in maintaining or undermining the overall integrity of a larger project management plan.

PROJECT DESCRIPTION

The federal evaluation was a complex and rather ambitious undertaking. The project included eight different hospitals as sites where the effectiveness of four different models of physician peer review were to be evaluated. Each of these four peer review mechanisms conformed to the general process-based paradigm common in this area. The paradigm included four steps: (1) identifying criteria or standards for good care (usually for specific patient conditions); (2) judging the adequacy of care by comparing how well existing care matched the standards; (3) when deficiencies in care were found, using some corrective action to change physician behavior so that care would more closely conform to the standards; and (4) after an appropriate lapse of time, reassessing the process of care to evaluate the success of the corrective actions. Thus, the peer review interventions that were being evaluated were basically different types of quality control mechanisms carried out by physicians on other physicians. In this particular study, the differences in the peer review mechanisms being tested were related to *when* the actual judgment of the adequacy of care was being made, either retrospectively or concurrently.

Thus, two hospitals implemented retrospective review, two hospitals implemented concurrent review, and two hospitals implemented combined retrospective and concurrent review. These three models all utilized the same explicit criteria for good care which were developed by physicians through a process of consensual judgment. The fourth model, a control, differed from these structured, explicit criteria models. Physicians in the last two hospitals performed retrospective review on the basis of implicit criteria (i.e., the internalized standards) that they as experienced clinicians used when judging the goodness of care.

In order for these peer review mechanisms to operate in each hospital, it was necessary to collect detailed data on the process of patient care—that is, what was actually done for the patient during the hospitalization episode. Because of the different models of peer review, these data had to be collected both concurrently and retrospectively. As part of the intervention, each hospital used its own process-of-care data in order to perform peer review according to the model to which that hospital had been randomly assigned.

In addition to designing and implementing the interventions, the major purpose of this evaluation project was to determine whether and how these different peer review mechanisms were functioning to improve the quality of patient care. The overall evaluation design required cross-hospital comparisons of the process-of-care data to see whether the review mechanisms were changing physician behavior so that it was in closer compliance with the criteria for good care. These process-of-care data included those used in the peer review at each hospital. The overall evaluation design also involved collecting patient outcome data from each hospital in order to determine whether the introduction of review mechanisms produced changes in patients' health.

The operational aspects of the project involved an average of four full-time data collectors and one part-time physician for each of eight hospitals, in addition to the activities of a central research and support staff of approximately ten persons. Although the project had made notable progress with the interventions in place and beginning to function, it continued to be plagued by project management and data problems that were of such magnitude as to result in its termination.

The fate of this project was not the result of any single factor, including data management problems. However, a comprehensive examination of all of the contributing factors is clearly beyond the scope of this chapter. The emphasis on the project's data management problems stems from the belief in their overall importance. Such problems occur frequently and can reduce significantly the quality of a study affected by them.

Data Activities

Since a data management plan should address the major issues of data collection, processing, and quality control (Sechrest, 1976), it will be useful to describe this evaluation project in these terms before discussing the data problems that arose. In this project, patient-specific data were being collected for 25 different medical and surgical conditions that were being used for peer review. The total patient-specific data set included the following measures:[1]

(1) *Standard demographic data.*

(2) *Identification of the patient's condition:* the patient's principal diagnosis defined as the reason for the patient's admission to the hospital.

(3) *Utilization data:* length of stay and the frequency and identity of lab tests, diagnostic and therapeutic procedures, surgery, consultations, and so on.

(4) *Process-of-care data:* measures of whether care for a particular case complied with both the procedures and timing requirements set by the criteria for that condition. For example, a typical condition could require over 60 elements of care.

(5) *Condition-specific outcome data:* measures of clinical indicators of proximate outcome.

(6) *Generalized outcome data:* patients' reports of their functional status—that is, their abilities in the area of mobility, physical

activities, social activities, and self-care activities—at the time of discharge.

(7) *Patient satisfaction data:* patients' reports of their assessment of and satisfaction with their care at the time of discharge.

All of the process-of-care data, along with the utilization data, demographic data, identification of the patient's condition, and most of the condition-specific outcome data, were collected retrospectively from an archival data source—the patient's medical record. Because of the different models of peer review, all of the process-of-care data were also collected concurrently from the patient's chart during his or her hospitalization. The rest of the measures necessary for the patient-specific data set—namely, measures of generalized health and satisfaction with care—were unavailable from any existing data source. Collection of these data at the time of the patient's discharge from the hospital required an interviewer to contact the patient just prior to his or her departure from the hospital to administer one questionnaire and request cooperation in completing another self-administered questionnaire. Additional follow-up outcome measures were collected after discharge by a telephone interviewer.

Personnel. Two types of personnel served as data collectors for this project. One group of persons with medical records training was based in the medical records department of each of the eight hospitals involved in the study. These personnel were responsible for abstracting utilization data from the chart of each patient who was discharged from the hospital. They were also responsible for identifying which of these discharges were patients who had any of the 25 surgical and medical diagnoses that were included as conditions for peer review. For these discharges, they had to abstract additional data—the required process-of-care data for that particular condition.

The other type of personnel who collected data for the project were master's-level nurses who were based in each of the eight hospitals involved in the study. The nurses were responsible for reviewing all hospital admissions and identifying which of these admissions were patients who had any of the 25 surgical and medical diagnoses included as conditions for peer review. For these admissions they had to abstract concurrently the required process-of-care data. This involved reviewing the hospitalized patients' charts almost daily in order to determine whether their care complied with the standards for good care. The nurses also collected additional sources of data through face-to-face interviews. These were the generalized measures of the patients' health, the functional status measure. This was required just prior to patients' discharge from the hospital, at which time the nurses also introduced and distributed the self-administered patient satisfaction questionnaires.

All process-of-care data—retrospective and concurrent—and the outcome measures were collected on specially prepared data collection forms that were compatible with data entry using terminals based in each hospital. The concurrent patient data forms had to be linked with the retrospective data collection forms for the same patient, prior to data entry, so that all data for one patient could be entered as a single case. All data collectors were trained and supervised by a member of the central project staff. Supervisors used site visits to each of the hospitals to review the quality of the data collectors' work, and telephone contact to facilitate problem-solving.

DATA MANAGEMENT PROBLEMS

Some health services evaluations present little in the way of difficulties in data management. Examples are studies that do not include primary data collection and use data from documents that are already in machine-readable form, or studies that require only data from a single questionnaire. However, as the above discussion may have indicated, there were a number of characteristics of the data set required for this project that presented the possibility, if not the likelihood, of difficulties in data management: (1) The absolute size of the data set was quite large; for example, a particular case could contain as many as 1,250 data elements, and some data elements were being collected on approximately 40,000 cases per year. (2) The major source of much of the data, namely hospital records, was known to have many shortcomings; the question has often been raised as to whether one should reasonably expect to abstract reliable information from the average medical record (Murnaghan and White, 1971). (3) The necessity to acquire comparable data from each of eight hospitals was problematic, since there was not complete uniformity in the hospital record systems. (4) The necessity to link as many as six different data sources from the same patient (i.e., admission interviews, concurrently abstracted patient data, discharge interviews and questionnaires, follow-up out-of-hospital interviews, and retrospectively abstracted patient data) introduced additional complexity.

Somewhat less obvious but equally threatening for ease of data management were characteristics of the hospitals and the hospital-based data collection personnel that produced problems: (1) the hospital environments in which data were being collected turned out to be difficult to control and posed many barriers to efficient operations. (2) The highly structured and redundant nature of certain of the data collection tasks proved unpopular with many of the perhaps overqualified data collection personnel. This led to morale and cooperation problems and eventually to declines in productivity.

Coding

What developed in this particular evaluation project were two data management problems of considerable severity. The abstraction of data from the patient's medical record often proved to be a complicated task. Many problems occurred because of difficulties and inadequacies in the record itself—ambiguous information, contradictory information, illegibility, and so forth. Also, an already complicated task was made more so by inadequate guidelines and training in the use of data collection forms, and some unnecessary complexity in these forms. The situation was worsened by lack of on-site supervision and the inability of the data collection supervisors to travel to the eight different hospitals frequently enough to monitor comprehensively the quality of the data collection process. In addition, working conditions at the hospitals were often not conducive to the task at hand. For example, there was often a lack of quiet work space and competing demands to perform other nonproject-related tasks. All of these problems helped create rather high error rates and/or low productivity in many of the hospitals.

It may be helpful to describe some of the types of problems that occurred in abstracting data from the medical records. While all of these problems occurred in the project under discussion, they are relevant to others as well. Since a medical record often seems to be a bundle of disorganized forms and notes, it was very common for abstractors' search techniques to be inadequate and for them to miss data that were present in the record (Hendrickson and Myers, 1973; Cayten, 1978).

Conversely, it was not uncommon for abstractors to use an inappropriate source of data. For example, they often mistakenly construed clinical indicators from a physical exam as part of the patient's history (Cayten, 1978). Such interpretation problems were frequent since judgments were often required when there was not exact agreement between the wording on the data collection form and what was in the medical record (Institute of Medicine, 1976). In some cases, errors arose because there was a poor understanding of certain medical terminology (Institute of Medicine, 1976). For example, in the case of concussion, the justification for patient's admission required an indication of both closed head trauma and an altered level of consciousness. Some abstractors incorrectly assumed that a notation of lacerations indicated that the head trauma was not "closed." A similar problem adding unnecessary complexity was introduced by the data collection forms. For example, in the case of inguinal hernia, the form included a conditional question which asked whether a "bulge" in the groin were present and, if so, whether the hernia were noted to be "reducible." The problem here was that the term "bulge" is not common medical terminology and the record often included no mention of bulge but did discuss reducibility. Thus the data collector, if following the form literally, would incorrectly indicate no physical evidence of the hernia.

Selection of cases according to the principal diagnosis was prone to error because of differences in how it can be defined. The principal diagnosis can be viewed as explaining admission, as being primarily responsible for the hospital stay, or as causing the illness episode (Murnaghan and White, 1971). Along the same lines, some confusion was introduced, since data collection guidelines in certain cases had to be site-specific because hospitals often had idiosyncratic definitions and procedures (Donabedian, 1969).

Completion Rate

The other major data management problem concerned the completion rate for the interviewer-administered generalized health measure. As mentioned earlier, administering this highly structured and redundant instrument was an unpopular task among the master's-level nurses. In addition, it was often very difficult for these nurses to get enough advance notice that a patient was about to be discharged to be able to contact and interview the patient. Apparently it was not uncommon for physicians to write discharge orders rather suddenly, and for patients to waste no time in leaving the hospital. Due to a combination of the nurses' lack of enthusiasm and some difficult situational constraints, the completion rate for this interview in some of the hospitals fell to an unacceptably low level, producing a significant nonresponse bias. For example, one hospital was not completing 80 percent of these interviews.

Another factor that probably magnified these problems was the limited ability of central project staff to monitor comprehensively the accuracy and completeness of the data. The total data management plan placed heavy reliance on an automated entry system that had a substantial set of built-in error checks and presumably had the ability to provide up-to-date production figures. Unfortunately, this system was never fully operational during the project's existence, and extensive backlogging of the data entry process occurred. This produced the associated problem of limited availability of information for data quality control purposes.

GUIDELINES FOR ASSURING DATA QUALITY

The evaluation literature does not include very many detailed discussions of basic issues in research management, particularly those dealing with data. Notable exceptions to this statement are found in publications that have a very practical orientation. These include Riecken and Boruch's (1974) *Social Experimentation,* the U.S. General Accounting Office's (1978) draft report entitled "Assessing Social Program Impact Evaluations: A Checklist Approach," and Sechrest's (1976) draft report, "Guidelines for Preparation of NCHSR Research Grant Applications." Perhaps this supports the contention that academic social scientists continue to display a general disinterest in the practical problems of research management. While the guidelines suggested here and in the above reports may be considered a somewhat basic approach, it is surprising how many research proposals with complex data requirements continue to pay no attention at all to a data management plan that includes data collection, data-processing, and data quality control. The last and in some ways most essential issue, data quality control, is probably most often not addressed. Riecken and Boruch (1974) suggest that this area is often ignored because it is tedious, intellectually unrewarding, and may involve overtones of suspicion. Whatever the reasons, it would seem that any research project that involves data of much complexity—and this is often the case with quality-of-care studies in health services research—could profit from explicit attention to the following issues.

Personnel Issues

Particularly in the case of archival data, the accuracy and completeness of the data source contribute substantially to the validity of any data collected from it. This issue has received enough attention to suggest some reservations about the reliability and validity of data entered into medical records (see Fessel and Van Brunt, 1972; Koran, 1975). However, such discussion is beyond the scope of this chapter. Besides the source of data, the data collection personnel—their competence, training, and supervision—are essential elements to maintaining the quality of data being collected in terms of accuracy and completeness.

Qualifications. Data collection personnel should have background and experience that are well matched to the requirements of the task they are to perform. Such qualifications should be defined thoughtfully and adhered to in recruiting personnel. For data collection from medical records, personnel require a knowledge of medical terminology, abbreviations, and formats; and, depending on the complexity of the task, they may require some clinical experience and the ability to make clinical judgments. Either persons with experience and training in medical records or persons with clinical training and experience may prove suitable for such data collection tasks. However, because there are various degrees in these areas and because educational background is not enough to assure good performance in the data collection tasks, certain other considerations should be included. Successful performance of related tasks in another research project may be the best predictor of successful performance. However, since personnel with that qualification may not be available, care should be taken to assure that the person understands that the task requires careful, almost compulsive attention to detail, and often limited outlet for any creativity. The discipline to perform a "paper and pencil" task that includes many highly standardized activities, repeatedly and consistently, may not be just what many nurses are looking for.

Those responsible for supervising the data collection personnel must be experienced and have the expertise, background, and maturity to serve as models for the data collection task. While infallibility is not expected in the case of data collection from medical records, supervisory personnel should be quite able to serve as "expert" reabstractors to assess the quality of the original data collector's performance. The demands of this position should not be underestimated. For example, in the evaluation project described here, this position required fairly extensive clinical knowledge, good judgment, ability to work with eight different hospital record systems, and detailed familiarity with over 25 different data collection forms.

Training. Once personnel have been selected, a certain amount of orientation and training will be necessary, depending on the complexity of the data collection task. This training should be rigorous enough to produce data collectors who can perform their tasks to a preset criterion of acceptable performance. For example, in the case of abstracting data from medical records, a requirement could be set for a specified number of error-free performances of abstracting and coding data within a specified time period.

Supervision. As noted in the GAO document (1978: 24) "adequate supervision is essential to identify those employees who are performing satisfactorily, those who need retaining, and those who must be replaced." This statement implies that performance levels must be assessed frequently to assure acceptable work. The information should be gathered and used, even if it requires firing and replacing personnel.

Quality Control

In addition to the need for competent personnel with high levels of training and supervision, structured procedures are necessary to review and maintain a prespecified level of data accuracy and completeness. These should be built into the overall project management plan and will vary depending on the exact data-related tasks. However, a reasonable way to determine what structured procedures to use is to examine all the data-related tasks and identify all the points where errors can occur (see Harris and Hoffman, 1975; Brooks and Bailar, 1978). For example, consider the case of the evaluation project described above. The first point where errors could occur was in the identification of any of the 25 medical or surgical study condition cases; errors here could be errors of omission or errors of commission. Next, information that was abstracted from the medical record and coded on the data collection form could be in error for any number of reasons. The interviewer-completed and patient-completed questionnaires could contain missing data and/or coding errors. The linkage of all or any of the data collection forms for a particular patient could be in error. Finally, errors could be introduced when all the data for a particular case were entered into the terminal. For these tasks, procedures can be selected to make data collection and processing as error-free and unbiased as possible.

The major procedures used in this particular project were verification of the data collectors' abstracting from the medical record through a sample reabstracting by the supervisors; built-in edit checks (consistency checks, range checks, and skip pattern or routing checks) in the automated data entry process; and automated checks to ensure that a particular case included all the required data collection forms for a particular patient. However, some of these procedures had not been built into the original project design and, as was described, data quality became a major problem.

Interpretation Problems. Almost every large-scale project will have to make at least some minor modifications in the data collection forms and/or guidelines, often as a result of unanticipated details or because of outright errors. An agreed-upon, structured procedure should be used so that interpretation problems are solved rapidly. The solution or decision and its justification should be documented in writing and disseminated to all data collectors. Without such explicit procedures, large-scale projects run the risk of introducing yet another potential source of error and inconsistency into the data collection process.

Clarity and simplicity in data collection forms can go a long way toward facilitating high-quality performance. Producing such forms for complex data sets requires some experience with formatting and questionnaire development, along with sufficient clinical expertise to avoid ambiguous medical terminology. If one person does not possess all of these skills, review by numerous persons, each with some of the required expertise, should improve the product—but at the cost of reduced efficiency. Pilot-testing of forms remains an essential correction device.

Scheduling. Most projects seem to fall behind schedule for a variety of reasons. In the case of data management, efforts should be made to adhere to realistic schedules within reasonable limits. Extensive backlogging of data collection should be recognized as a very serious sign and should be corrected as rapidly as possible, even if this requires modifications in the overall design of the project. Rigid adherence to procedures that are not working, in the hope that things will get better, will probably prove to be an extremely costly mistake.

In a large-scale data collection effort, one should set the requirement that some of the data be available in final form in the early stages of data collection. This will allow preliminary analyses that can assist in monitoring the accuracy and completeness of the data. Such data can also be used in assessing certain problems in the general analysis plan for the project. The advantage of these early analyses is, of course, related to the fact that changes in the data management plan and other operations will still be possible.

External Staff. While most large-scale projects have advisory boards, it may be useful to consider more detailed, ongoing critical evaluation of the actual operations of a project. Perhaps the model of the concurrent meta-evaluator discussed by Cook and Gruder (1979) could be considered as a useful back-up source for assessing and assuring quick solutions to data management problems.

The organizational location of data collection personnel should also be considered carefully. Hospital personnel will often be recommended for employment on a project that is collecting data from the medical records in that hospital. It is possible that accepting such an arrangement will allow project management to have limited or nonexistent control over the work quality and productivity of such personnel. If this is the case, this arrangement should be actively avoided.

Selection of data-processing equipment and methods should be based on advice from persons with extensive technical and research experience. Well-tested methods should be selected. The most sophisticated system will not be helpful if it requires unavailable resources and cannot be operated in a timely fashion.

Error Rates. While there surely are many more mechanisms to help in assuring data quality, monitoring is critical. It is important to monitor data quality closely enough that systematic sources of error will be detected. Evaluators doing impact evaluations are likely to consider error rates (and the issue of the unreliability of measures) in terms of threats to statistical conclusion validity. The general perception may be that most errors in data collection add a random error component, thus increasing the variance of one's estimates, making small effects more difficult to detect, and no-difference findings more likely. However, the possibility of data collector error being a systematic source of error that can actually bias one's conclusions should not be ignored (see Hendrickson and Myers, 1973).

A decision regarding what is an acceptable error rate should be made during a project's planning stages. In many cases there may be no normative information or agreement on what this rate should be. Despite the fact that there may not yet be much detailed information of this sort available, a research manager will have to consider the tradeoffs between the increased costs necessary to produce lower error rates and the problems inherent in accepting higher error rates.

SUMMARY

This chapter has described a large-scale federal evaluation that encountered difficulties in data management. Two specific data collection tasks, abstracting data from medical records and interviewing patients about to be discharged, produced what were believed to be unacceptably high error rates. A number of practical guidelines were recommended to help assure high data quality. The essential components of a data management plan were discussed, with an emphasis on intense monitoring of data quality so that problems can be identified and corrected rapidly.

It should also be noted that a data management plan must be seen as one part of the total project management plan. It is essential that the total management plan be truly comprehensive and developed in full detail at the outset of a project. As part of this planning effort, special attention should be paid to incorporating mechanisms, such as those described above, to assure data quality.

NOTE

1. Actually, this discussion is restricted to those data that were collected retrospectively. Additional data were collected concurrently; other retrospective data were collected as control variables; and organizational data were also collected. However, these additional data are not discussed here, since they are not as relevant to this discussion of data management.

REFERENCES

BROOKS, C. A. and B. A. BAILAR (1978) "An error profile: employment as measured by the current population survey," in Statistical Policy Working Paper 3. Washington, DC: Government Printing Office.

CAYTEN, C. G. (1978) "Steps in index of injury/illness severity development." Emergency Medical Services (November-December): 103-106.

COOK, T. D. and C. GRUDER (1979) "Meta evaluation research," in L. Sechrest et al. (eds.) Evaluation Studies Review Annual, Volume 4. Beverly Hills, CA: Sage.

DONABEDIAN, A. (1969) Medical Care Appraisal-Quality and Utilization: A Guide to Medical Care Administration, Volume 2. New York: American Public Health Association.

FESSEL, W. J. and E. E. VAN BRUNT (1972) "Assessing quality of care from the medical record." New England Journal of Medicine 286: 134-138.

GILBERT, J. P., R. J. LIGHT, and F. MOSTELLER (1975) "Assessing social innovations: an empirical base for policy," in C. A. Bennett and A. A. Lumsdaine (eds.) Evaluation and Experiment. New York: Academic.

HARRIS, K. W. and K. HOFFMAN (1975) "Quality control in the hospital discharge survey." Vital & Health Statistics Publications Series 2, 68. Washington, DC: Government Printing Office.

HENDRICKSON, L. and J. MYERS (1973) "Some sources and potential consequences of errors in medical data recording." Methods of Information Medicine 12: 38-45.

Institute of Medicine (1976) "An assessment of the reliability of abstracted hospital utilization data: final report." Washington, DC: National Academy of Sciences.

KORAN, L. M. (1975) "The reliability of clinical methods, data and judgments." New England Journal of Medicine 293: 695-701.

MURNAGHAN, J. H. and K. L. WHITE (1971) "Hospital patient statistics problems and prospects." New England Journal of Medicine 284: 822-828.

RIECKEN, H. W. and R. F. BORUCH [eds.] (1974) Social Experimentation. New York: Academic.

SECHREST, L. (1976) "Guidelines for Preparation of NCHSR Research Grant Applications" (Draft for review). National Center for Health Services Research.

–– and R. Y. COHEN (1979) "Evaluating outcomes in health care," in G. C. Stone et al. (eds.) Health Psychology. San Francisco: Jossey-Bass.

U.S. General Accounting Office (1978) "Assessing social program impact evaluations: a checklist approach (exposure draft)."

3

Paul M. Wortman

University of Michigan

RANDOMIZED CLINICAL TRIALS

Randomized, controlled, clinical trials (RCTs) have been widely advocated in the health research area as the summum bonum of research methods (Byar et al., 1976; Cochrane, 1972), just as they have by evaluators in other areas (see Campbell and Stanley, 1966; Boruch, 1976). Although this methodology is not universally endorsed, it is nevertheless the preeminent one. In this chapter we will examine the role of RCTs in evaluating health services, particularly medical technologies. We will not be directly concerned with how RCTs are conducted (for that, see Cook and Campbell, 1979; Peto et al., 1976), but with some factors limiting their usefulness.

FREQUENCY OF RCT's

In light of the general support for this research methodology, what is the frequency of RCTs in health research? We would

AUTHOR'S NOTE: This chapter is based on a talk delivered at an ISR Tuesday noon lecture on March 25, 1980.

TABLE 3.1   Frequency of Randomized Clinical Trials (RCTs)

	Neurosurgery[a]	Cancer[b]
Years	1947-1977	1966-1971
Total	4685	2370
Clinical Trials	339 (7.3%)	252 (11.1%)
RCTs	11 (0.2%)	52 (2.2%)

a. articles in the *Journal of Neurosurgery* (adapted from Haines, 1979)
b. abstracts submitted to the American Association for Cancer Research (adapted from Chalmers et al., 1972)

expect it to be high given the above view, the relative ease of analyzing the data from an RCT, the accuracy of the statistical estimates produced, and the frequency with which large-scale, multicenter RCT evaluations are in the news. While it is not possible to examine all of the vast medical literature, some researchers have reported on the frequency of RCTs in a number of medical areas.

Haines (1979) examined all issues of the *Journal of Neurosurgery* during its first thirty years (see Table 1). Out of a total of 4685 articles 863 (18.4 percent) were evaluations of "diagnostic and therapeutic techniques." These were classified in turn as: (1) clinical reviews: 524 (60.7%); (2) uncontrolled clinical trials: 321 (37.2%); and (3) controlled clinical trials: 18 (2.1%). Thus, only 339 articles (7.3%) were clinical trials. Of the controlled clinical trials, 11 were RCTs (0.2%) and only one involved a double-blind procedure. As Haines notes, "only one article fulfilled the criteria for a satisfactory randomized clinical trial."

Similarly, Chalmers et al. (1972) reviewed all the abstracts published from the annual meetings of the American Association for Cancer Research during the 1965-1971 period (see Table 3.1). Again, they found relatively few RCTs of drug therapies. Out of 2370 published abstracts, only 52 (2.2%) were RCTs. Finally, a recently reported survey of 612 randomly selected research studies published in three leading medical journals from 1946 to 1976 revealed an optimistic trend in the quality methodology employed (Fletcher and Fletcher, 1979). Clinical trials increased from 13 to 21 percent of all studies, while RCTs increased from zero to 5 percent.

In sum, RCTs account for a modest but growing amount of the research designs used by health researchers. Whether this trend will continue as its advocates urge will depend on a number of factors. Although practical and political factors should not be ignored (see Conner, 1977; Patton et al., 1977), we agree with Weiss (1973) among others that the utilization of research, especially evaluations, is of critical importance. Thus, in the remainder of this chapter we will consider the utility of RCTs in the evaluation of medical innovation.

UTILIZATION OF RCTs

Gastric Freezing

We begin our examination of this issue with a recent but already classic case from the annals of medical research—gastric "freezing." This innovation was like a shooting star in the firmament of medical technology. In the brief span of seven years from 1962 to 1969, it was announced, adopted, and finally abandoned. What is gastric freezing, and what role did RCTs play in determining the fate of this innovation?

Gastric freezing was a treatment for duodenal ulcer, a chronic health condition that is thought to cause 10,000 deaths per year. The problem is believed to result, in part, from increased levels of stomach or gastric acid. In the early 1960s there was no known effective treatment. Patients with severe symptoms such as bleeding ulcers often had surgery. This was a risky treatment with high rates of mortality and recurrence. Then, in 1962, Owen Wangensteen, a surgeon affiliated with the University of Minnesota, announced an apparent cure for this problem.

Wangensteen's technique involved freezing or cooling the stomach. This was accomplished through a simple procedure in which a patient swallowed a balloon that was positioned in the stomach and then filled with a coolant. The procedure lasted about one hour. Wangensteen and his associates (1962) claimed "dramatic" results in the reduction of gastric secretions and pain. They viewed the technique as a safe and inexpensive alternative to surgery.

This report created tremendous interest and excitement among the medical community and the public as well. Duodenal ulcer accounted for the vast majority of ulcer cases, and gastric freezing appeared to be a major breakthrough in its treatment. Within the next two years the technique was widely disseminated, and over 1500 gastric freezing machines were sold (Fineberg, 1979).

The research methodology used in the early studies of gastric freezing, including Wangensteen's, was mainly observational. For example, Wangensteen based his claims on the results of ten patients who were subjected to the latest freezing procedure. As Campbell and Stanley (1966) have noted, such case studies are open to a variety of alternative interpretations or "plausible rival hypotheses." Thus, it was not surprising that the initial enthusiasm for the procedure was soon followed by serious doubts concerning its efficacy and safety. Members of the American Gastroenterological Association, gathered at its annual meeting in May 1963, concurred. They recommended that approval of the gastric freezing technique be withheld until appropriate evidence was available. To obtain it, they initiated a multicenter, cooperative, double-blind RCT (Ruffin et al., 1969).

The RCT was an impressive and methodologically sophisticated study. Five leading medical schools participated, and a careful, uniform procedure was developed. This involved the use of identical criteria for patient selection, procedure for treatment, data collection, and analysis. In order to identify placebo effects and to blind the study as well, a "sham procedure" was devised as a control. This procedure was identical to the feeezing technique, except that the coolant did not enter the balloon. Instead, two small auxiliary tubes were used to fill the balloon with tap water at body temperature. The study involved 160 patients observed over a two-year period. The results of the study were quite definitive. As Ruffin and his associates (1969: 16) note in the abstract of their article,

[they] demonstrate conclusively that the "freezing" procedure is no better than the sham in the treatment of duodenal ulcer. . . . It is reasonable to assume that the relief of pain and subjective improvement reported by early investigators were probably due to the psychologic effect of the procedure.

It would appear that this RCT, in fact, provided the *coup de grace* for gastric freezing. This view is supported by Miao (1977) in her review of gastric freezing (see the lefthand side of Table 3.2). She views it as a shining example of what Weiss (1977) calls "instrumental utilization"—the direct application of research findings. While Weiss does not believe in this type of utilization, here, apparently, was a nice counterexample. Unfortunately, Fineberg's extensive investigation (1979) of gastric freezing led him to a quite different opinion of the utility of the cooperative RCT on gastric freezing (see the righthand side of Table 3.2). Fineberg claims that the technique was abandoned "without compelling evidence in the literature that the procedure was inefficacious."

Relationship Between Methodology and Outcome. How can one explain these contradictory views? Perhaps one way is to examine the patterns of evidence for and against gastric freezing published during this time. Both authors review the literature and develop tabular synopses. Miao lists 22 studies and Fineberg 33. Fineberg also provides evaluative information on the studies and indicates how the outcomes changed with time. As can be seen in Table 3.3, support for the innovation diminished over time, with no "favorable" studies appearing after 1963 and, with the exception of one study, almost totally negative evaluations from 1965 on.

TABLE 3.2   Two Views on the Randomized Clinical Trial
of Gastric "Freezing"

Miao (1977)	*Fineberg (1979)*
"Through the collaborative effort on a carefully randomized investigation, the physicians reached a consensus whereupon the use of gastric freezing for the treatment of duodenal ulcer was discontinued. *This process is an example of the medical profession's successfully evaluating and regulating the use of its own innovative treatments"* (p. 209, emphasis added).	"Results of this major study did not appear in the literature until 1969. *The report was unequivocal in its negative conclusions, but of little practical consequence, as if a marble tombstone were erected over the grave of a patient already several years deceased"* (p. 188, emphasis added).

TABLE 3.3   Overall Evaluation of Gastric Freezing by
Clinical Studies[a]

Year	Favorable	*Qualified Favorable*	*Neutral*	*Qualified Unfavorable*	*Unfavorable*
1962	OOO				
1963	O	OOOOO		O	
1964		OOOR	OOO	O	OOR
1965		R[b]	OO	O	
1966			C		OC
1967				R	R
1968					
1969				O	R

O = observed/uncontrolled study
C = controlled study
R = randomized, double-blind study

a. adapted from Fineberg (1979: 185)
b. performed by Wangensteen

TABLE 3.4   The Relationship Between Design Quality and Outcome: Gastric Freezing

Degree of Control	Degree of "Enthusiasm"			Totals
	Marked	*Moderate*	*None*	
Well controlled		2	4	6
Poorly controlled			2	2
Uncontrolled	4	9	12	25
Totals	4	11	18	33

NOTE: adapted from Fineberg (1979)

Following the approach of Grace et al. (1966), we can also examine the relationship between design quality and the overall outcome. These are contained in Table 3.4. The table indicates that support or "enthusiasm" for the innovation is largely from the early, weaker, uncontrolled studies. Only two "well-controlled" studies produced "qualified" support for the innovation, and one of them was conducted by the developer of gastric freezing. The majority of the stronger studies are not supportive. Thus, by the time of the definitive 1969 paper by Ruffin and his associates, the negative pattern had been fairly well established. It is likely that the published evidence lags behind personal experience and underrepresents it. Fineberg et al. (1978) have shown that in some cases of innovation colleagues may be more influential than published articles, although the "opinion leaders" are research-oriented.

A related problem affecting the utilization of an RCT is the timing or fit between research and innovation. Here, although a definitive study was undertaken early on, the results were not timely and were even "too late" to do more than confirm an existing opinion. This has not always been the case, as Barsamian (1977) points out in his discussion of internal mammary artery ligation. In this case, two RCTs were conducted within a year of the innovation's announcement. As with gastric freezing, they demonstrated that the relief of angina claimed by proponents could be explained as a placebo effect.

Evidence for Other Innovations

Protacaval Shunt. Investigators have examined the pattern of evidence for other medical innovations. One of these involves the use of portacaval shunt operations for the treatment of bleeding esophageal varices. While the operation was introduced in 1945, it was not until 1965 that RCTs were used to determine if this surgery should be performed as a prophylactic procedure on those who had never bled. There was no difference in survival. As a consequence, the value of the procedure for those who had bled was reassessed and more RCTs were conducted. By 1974, the results indicated, according to Bunker et al. (1978), "at best slight survival value." The relationship between the findings and research methodology was summarized by Grace and his associates (1966) and updated by Gilbert et al. (1977). They are presented in Table 3.5.

The pattern is similar to that found for gastric freezing. Again, only six studies were "well controlled," and none indicated "marked" support for the innovation. The "poorly controlled" and "uncontrolled" studies generated nearly identical patterns of enthusiasm: 72 percent marked, 21 percent moderate, 6 percent none. These results indicate that poorly designed studies can create a false impression of strong support because of their sheer number. This is not only misleading, but may make it difficult to conduct well-designed studies (as we shall see below).

Electronic Fetal Monitoring. A final, more contemporary, example is drawn from our own work examining the research on electronic fetal monitoring (EFM). This is an obstetric technique developed during the 1960s. Monitoring today typically consists of measures of fetal heart rate obtained either externally by ultrasound or internally by electrodes attached to the

TABLE 3.5   The Relationship Between Design Quality and Outcome:
Portacaval Shunt

Degree of Control	Degree of "Enthusiasm"			Totals
	Marked	*Moderate*	*None*	
Well controlled	0	3	3	6
Poorly controlled	10	3	2	15
Uncontrolled	24	7	1	32
Totals	34	13	6	53

NOTE: from Gilbert et al. (1977: 686)

fetus and measures of blood acidity in a sample obtained from the fetal scalp. EFM was originally used in high-risk pregnancies, but it is increasingly employed in all deliveries. So rapid has its dissemination been that by 1976 a survey (reported by Banta and Thacker, 1979) found that 77 percent of physicians believe that all labors should be monitored electronically.

Only recently have controlled clinical trials on EFM been conducted. The results of these and other studies are reported in Tables 3.6 and 3.7. The temporal pattern of results again indicates increasing negative findings, especially from the RCTs. There are more controlled studies due to the frequent use of retrospective, historical controls—typically patients who were pregnant (or their records) prior to the adoption of EFM. As Thompson and Cohen (Chapter 6) note, this is confounded with a general decline in infant mortality that occurred during this period and was not caused by monitoring.

Thompson and Cohen discuss the various negative outcomes or risks associated with EFM. The major risk is an increase in cesarean section rate (CSR). Banta and Thacker (1979) claim half of the recent increase in CSR—some 96,000—is a result of EFM. They estimate an increased cost of $2300 per cesarean section (a figure used by Thompson and Cohen) and an in-

TABLE 3.6   Overall Evaluation of Electronic Fetal Monitoring (EFM) by Clinical Studies

Year	Favorable	Qualified Favorable	Neutral	Qualified Unfavorable	Unfavorable
1970	O				
1971					
1972	CC				
1973	OOCCC				
1974	CCC		C		
1975	OCCCC	C	C	CC	
1976	OCCCCC	OR[a]	O	C	R
1977	OCCCC		OO	O	
1978	CC	C		R	
1979					R

O = observed/uncontrolled study
C = controlled study
R = randomized clinical trial

a. More cesarean sections for monitored patients

TABLE 3.7   The Relationship Between Design Quality and Outcome: Electronic Fetal Monitoring

Degree of Control	Degree of "Enthusiasm"			Totals
	Marked	Moderate	None	
Well controlled	0	1	3	4
Poorly controlled	24[a]	2	5	31
Uncontrolled	6	1	4	11
Totals	30	4	12	46

a. There were 23 studies using historical controls.

creased risk of maternal mortality between three and thirty times that for a normal delivery.

The consistent patterns of evidence—early favorable, but methodologically weak, evidence followed by unfavorable, methodologically sound, evidence—raises the issue of timing once again. RCTs may be infeasible in a climate of opinion based on inadequate evidence. Physicians are likely to decline on ethical grounds to participate in an RCT if they believe these weak studies and are unwilling to withhold an apparent benefit from some patients. Ample evidence of this is already available. For example, Renou et al. (1976: 470-471), reporting the results of their RCT and EFM, note:

> During the course of the trial one of the [eight] doctors withdrew his patients . . . because he felt that intensive care was effective, and that it would be unethical for a high-risk patient to be managed without such care.

A similar statement appears in a report (Kloster et al., 1979) of an RCT on coronary bypass surgery. Commenting on the decreasing number of available patients for the study, the authors state that it "may have reflected attitudes of referring physicians regarding random assignment.

SOME METHODOLOGICAL PROBLEMS WITH RCTs

Power

We have seen that the absence of physician cooperation and patient attrition can hinder or even undermine an RCT. In her review of gastric freezing, Miao (1977) notes that many studies were improperly designed. Specifically, they had too few subjects to reject the null hypothesis (of no difference) if it were false—in statistical jargon, a Type II error. That is, the studies lacked statistical power (defined as 1 – the probability of a Type II error) usually resulting from too few subjects or patients. The problem of small sample size is, unfortunately, all too prevalent, as a recent, excellent paper by Freiman et al. (1978) notes. The authors examined 71 RCTs that failed to reject the null hypothesis. These "negative" studies were published in leading medical journals from 1960 to 1977. The investigators found that 67 of the trials did not have enough subjects to detect a 25 percent difference between experimental and control groups with power of .90 or better. Moreover, 57 of these studies contained this effect size in a 90 percent confidence interval.

Coronary Bypass Surgery

There are other methodological problems that have emerged as well. The recent and continuing controversy over the effectiveness of saphenous vein bypass graft for patients with chronic "stable" angina resulting from blocked coronary arteries is illustrative. The surgery was first introduced in 1967 and was almost immediately accepted, despite the absence of any convincing evidence of its effectiveness (McIntosh and Garcia, 1978). By 1970 an estimated 25,000 coronary-artery surgeries were performed (Paton, 1978). The number has continued to increase. The most recent figures (from 1978) indicate that over 70,000 bypass operations were being performed annually at a cost of $15,000 each (Star, 1878).

It was not until 1977 that the first RCT was reported. Why did it take so long? And why was such a costly, complicated, and risky procedure so rapidly adopted? Bunker et al. (1978) claim that there are a number of factors that influence the fast adoption of such innovations. They are identical to those we noted with respect to gastric freezing: a life-threatening condition with no alternative therapy available and dramatic results with a technique that makes sense physiologically. Warner (1975) has called this "desperation-reaction" diffusion. He adds that economic constraints need to be absent. Under these conditions it is easy to see how this surgical innovation became widely disseminated without RCTs. In fact, one of the developers is reported to have said it would be unethical to withhold the treatment from a control group.

Research Training. This indicates another problem that frequently delays the evaluation of medical innovations. The developers of such techniques are often strongly committed to their discoveries and are neither interested nor trained in the niceties of sound methodological assessment. This has been the case with gastric freezing, coronary artery bypass surgery, renal dialysis, and numerous other health innovations. As we have seen, this initiates a process where research is delayed or impeded by the false expectations generated by low-quality data.

As a consequence, the first RCT on coronary-artery bypass surgery was reported ten years after the introduction of this procedure (Murphy et al., 1977a). This cooperative, multicenter trial conducted by the Veterans Administration reported that

> there was no statistically significant difference in survival, at a minimal follow-up of 21 months, between patients treated medically and those treated with saphenous-vein-bypass grafting. At 36 months, 87% of the medical group and 88% of the surgical group were alive.

The study created a controversy that still continues. The immediate reaction—both favorable and unfavorable—was so great that the *New England Journal of Medicine* in 1977 published a "Special Correspondence" section containing twelve letters and replies by the authors and the editor.

Efficacy. The VA study was attacked on many grounds. One of the major criticisms concerned the quality of the surgery performed at the VA hospitals. The operative mortality rate of 5.6 percent was much higher than that of many leading surgical centers, where about 1.5 percent mortality was more common. Moreover, the patency rate of the bypass grafts (i.e., the proportion unobstructed) was lower than in other medical centers. Both of these measures indicate that the trial lacked "integrity" (Sechrest and Redner, forthcoming) or, as it is more commonly called in the health area, "efficacy" (Office of Technology Assessment, 1978). That is, the study was not conducted "under ideal conditions."

Moving Target Problem. Again, time is an important component of this criticism. It could be that the treatment did not meet existing standards or standards in effect when the study was published. For coronary-artery bypass, the latter was the case. As one critical letter (Boncheck and Brooks, 1977) noted, "it is . . . important to avoid comparing current medical results with outdated and inadequate surgical results." Thus, the rate of technological development (Greer, 1979), or the so-called moving target problem (Wagner, 1979), may be viewed as invalidating the relevance of an RCT. Innovations are characterized by rapid change that may limit the usefulness of an RCT by quickly making the evaluation obsolete. However, as Braunwald (1977) observed in his reply to the critics, medical treatment of coronary-artery disease is also improving, and it will require other RCTs to settle this dispute. Our preliminary coding of these studies reveals a pattern of evidence similar to those illustrated above in Tables 3.3 and 3.6. In this case, however, the results shift from "favorable" to "no difference" or "neutral" over time.

Other criticisms leveled at the VA study included those leveled at the use of different patient criteria for admission into the study at various sites. Along with similar differences in surgical skill, this intersite variation was claimed as a threat to the internal validity of the study. This is an appropriate criticism and one that stirred much debate as physicians at some VA hospitals sought to protect their record of quality surgery. The authors of the study (Murphy et al., 1977b) replied that even when the sites with the highest surgical mortality rates were eliminated from the analysis—thereby lowering the mortality rate almost by half—there remained no statistical difference between the two treatments. However, it should be noted that this analysis may not have had sufficient statistical power to reject the null hypothesis.

Crossovers. Perhaps the most sticky methodological problem with the VA study concerned crossovers—patients assigned to one treatment who switch to another. Nonadherence to therapy involved "those who refused operation (18 of 286) and medical patients who later chose operation (54 of 310)." Thus, one out of every six patients assigned to medical therapy eventually crossed over into the surgical treatment—a point that was noted in a number of critical letters commenting on the study. In order to deal with this problem, the authors analyzed the data in the following four ways: "by original treatment assignment; by actual treatment received; by treatment assigned, deleting all nonadherers; and by treatment assigned, with each nonadherer being considered as lost to follow-up observation at the time of his treatment change." The authors reported that all these analyses produced "consistent results," showing no difference between the two therapeutic approaches.

The question confronting a methodologist is: Do these analyses provide an unbiased estimate of the effect of surgery? Unfortunately, the answer is "no." While the authors noted that the baseline characteristics of the crossovers were "comparable" to adherers, they admit in their reply to this criticism that over half could be considered "treatment failures" (Murphy et al., 1977b). This means that there was nonrandom attrition of the least favorable patients in the medically treated group, and it introduces a systematic bias into the data that cannot be corrected by the analyses employed.

In the first instance, the authors followed the strategy recommended by Riecken et al. (1974) and analyzed the data by treatment assignment. While this preserves randomization, it does so at the cost of weakening the integrity of the treatments. The consequent loss of construct validity (Cook and Campbell, 1979) means that the medical group contains a sizable number of patients who, in fact, received surgery. As we have just noted, these contained a majority of the cases with the worst prognosis. It appears that the survival of these patients may have been improved through surgery. Thus, it is possible that the mean survival of the medically treated group has been artificially raised by this analytic approach.

The second approach taken by the authors gets around the problem of construct validity by analyzing the data by treatment received. However, it does this at the price of randomization. The quasi-experiment that results has the medically treated group pruned of those at greatest risk (i.e., the crossovers), while simultaneously the surgical group is burdened with them. This would almost certainly raise the mean survival for the former group while possibly lowering it for the latter. Again, the analysis might conceal a real effect for surgery.

The last two strategies are no better. The removal of nonadherers still improves the medically treated group. Finally, keeping patients' data in the analysis until they cross over only implies increasing bias with time. But since survival is being examined, it is of little value. As a consequence, there is systematic bias in all four analysis methods toward finding no difference between the two therapeutic modalities.

Secondary analysis or replication of the study could resolve this and the other problems. The VA study has, in fact, been replicated (Kloster et al., 1979). While most of the problems raised with the VA study were corrected in this RCT, there was still a high rate of crossovers among medically treated patients—8 of 49 patients. It appears that this is a persistent type of attrition that warrants special methodological attention. One approach to secondary analysis would investigate the consequences of such a treatment shift. This could be done by assuming surgery improves health by about 25 percent and determining whether removal of the worst sixth of the medically treated patients obscures this effect. At present, it is only possible to speculate that a potential effect is being hidden by patient attrition.[1]

Political Problems

Even where reanalysis may validate or vindicate the original findings, it may not be sufficient to persuade proponents of the innovation that it should be abandoned or limited. The prolonged controversy over the University Group Diabetes Project (UGDP) attests to the political problems an RCT can encounter (Kolata, 1979).

The UGDP was designed to test the effectiveness of oral antidiabetes drugs, specifically tolbutamide and phenformin. Both drugs were eventually dropped from the study because they appeared toxic and led to deaths from a variety of causes (e.g., cardiovascular complications for tolbutamide). The FDA reacted to this UGDP action by moving to have warning labels placed on all oral antidiabetic drugs. This was strongly opposed by a small group of diabetologists. They attacked the integrity of the study and the reputation of the biostatistician in charge of collecting and analyzing the data. They also hired a lawyer who has succeeded in blocking the FDA's attempt to insert warning labels for the last ten years.

As a consequence of this heated controversy, the director of the National Institutes of Health asked the Biometric Society, the professional association for biostatisticians, to review the UGDP findings. After four years of examination, including reanalysis, it issued a report supporting the original findings. Nevertheless, the attacks on the study persist, and other charges have been made, such as poor data handling and improper patient treatment.

CONCLUSIONS

What can we conclude, or at least hypothesize, based on this brief and selective review of the role of randomization in health research? First, RCTs are obviously important and more are needed, but other factors also influence their impact. Timing is perhaps the single most critical factor affecting the value of an RCT, and one that poses a dilemma. If the trial is too soon, it may evaluate a primitive form of the technology that is obsolete when the report is published. On the other hand, if the evaluation comes too late, it may be either superfluous (as in gastric freezing) or encounter entrenched opposition (as in the oral antidiabetes drug study).

Second, we need to be able to predict which medical innovations are likely to succeed. If evaluative testing is done too early, the social costs may be too high, since most innovations do not work out. Are the patterns of evidence described above sufficiently different for "successes" and "failures" to allow targeted evaluations?

Finally, there are methodological issues that need attention. Can the so-called poorly controlled quasi-experimental studies be aggregated to predict the outcomes of RCTs? There is currently much interest in data aggregation methods (see Glass,

1977; Pillemer and Light, 1980). Can acceptable methods for handling crossovers or other types of attrition be developed? We have outlined one approach, but it needs to be applied and refined along with other procedures.

In the field of health, the costs of faulty innovation are high. Both precious lives and resources depend on the adequacy of the information available. As we have seen, this is often lacking. Health, unlike other areas, holds pressures for innovation and cures that are immense. While some regulatory mechanisms are in place and others are being proposed, it is the quality of the evaluations that are essential. Only by insisting on methodological quality can quality of care be assured.

NOTE

1. However, a third study with 116 patients with stable angina (Mathur and Guinn, 1977) is available in which few (4 of 60 medically treated) failed to adhere to treatment assignment. It, too, found no statistically significant difference in mortality and nonfatal infarcts between the two groups, although there were more among the medically treated patients. Again, statistical power is a concern.

REFERENCES

BANTA, H. D. and S. B. THACKER (1979) "Costs and benefits of electronic fetal monitoring: a review of the literature," in NCHSR Research Report Series, DHEW Publication (PHS) 79-3245, Washington, DC: Government Printing Office.
BARSAMIAN, E. M. (1977) "The rise and fall of internal mammary artery ligation in the treatment of angina pectoris and the lessons learned," in J. P. Bunker et al. (eds.) Costs, Risks, and Benefits of Surgery. New York: Oxford University Press.
BONCHEK, L. I. and H. L. BROOKS (1977) "Special correspondence." New England Journal of Medicine 297: 1466-1467.
BORUCH, R. F. (1976) "On common contentions about randomized field experiments," in G. V Glass (ed.) Evaluation Studies Review Annual, Volume 1. Beverly Hills, CA: Sage.
BRAUNWALD, E. (1977) "Special correspondence." New England Journal of Medicine 297: 1469-1470.
BUNKER, J. P., D. HINKLEY, and W. V. McDERMOTT (1978) "Surgical innovation and its evaluation." Science 200: 937-941.

BYAR, D. P., R. M. SIMON, W. T. FRIEDEWALD, J. J. SCHLESSELMAN, D. L. DEMETS, J. H. ELLENBERG, M. H. GAIL, and J. H. WARE (1976) "Randomized clinical trials: perspectives on some recent ideas." New England Journal of Medicine 195: 74-80.

CAMPBELL, D. T. and J. STANLEY (1966) Experimental and Quasi-Experimental Designs for Research. Skokie, IL: Rand McNally.

CHALMERS, T. C., J. B. BLOCK, and S. LEE (1972) "Controlled studies in clinical cancer research." New England Journal of Medicine 287: 75-78.

COCHRANE, A. L. (1972) Effectiveness and Efficiency: Random Reflections on Health Services. London: Burgess.

CONNER, R. F. (1977) "Selecting a control group: an analysis of the randomization process in twelve social reform programs." Evaluation Quarterly 1: 195-244.

COOK, T. D. and D. T. CAMPBELL (1979) Quasi-Experimentation: Design and Analysis Issues for Field Settings. Skokie, IL: Rand McNally.

FINEBERG, H. V. (1979) "Gastric freezing—a study of diffusion of a medical innovation," Appendix D in Medical Technology and the Health Care System. Washington, DC: National Academy of Sciences.

———, R. A. GABEL, and M. B. SOSMAN (1978) "Acquisition and application of new medical knowledge by anesthesiologists." Anesthesiology 48: 430-436.

FLETCHER, R. H. and S. W. FLETCHER (1979) "Clinical research in general medical journals: a 30-year perspective." New England Journal of Medicine 301: 180-183.

FREIMAN, J. A., T. C. CHALMERS, H. SMITH, and R. R. KUEBLER (1978) "The importance of beta, the Type II error and sample size in the design and interpretation of the randomized control trial." New England Journal of Medicine 299: 690-694.

GILBERT, J. P., B. McPEEK, and F. MOSTELLER (1977) "Statistics and ethics in surgery and anesthesia." Science 198: 684-689.

GLASS, G. V (1977) "Integrating findings: the meta-analysis of research." Review of Research in Education 5: 351-379.

GRACE, N. D., H. MUENCH, and T. C. CHALMERS (1966) "The present status of shunts for portal hypertension in cirrhosis." Gastroenterology 50: 684-691.

GREER, A. L. (1979) Medical Technology: Assessment, Diffusion, and Implementation. Milwaukee: University of Wisconsin—Milwaukee Urban Research Center.

HAINES, S. J. (1979) "Randomized clinical trials in the evaluation of surgical innovation." Journal of Neurosurgery 51: 5-11.

KLOSTER, F. E., E. L. KREMKARE, L. W. RITZMANN, S. H. RAHIMTOOLA, J. ROSCH, and P. KANAREK (1979) "Coronary bypass for stable angina: a prospective randomized study." New England Journal of Medicine 300: 149-157.

KOLATA, G. B. (1979) "Controversy over study of diabetes drugs continues for nearly a decade." Science 203: 986-990.

MATHUR, V. S. and G. A. GUINN (1977) "Prospective randomized study of the surgical therapy of stable angina." Cardiovascular Clinics 8: 131-144.

McINTOSH, H. D. and J. A. GARCIA (1978) "The first decade of aortocoronary bypass grafting, 1967-1977: a review." Circulation 57: 405-431.

MIAO, L. L. (1977) "Gastric freezing: an example of the evaluation of medical therapy by randomized clinical trials," in J. P. Bunker et al. (eds.) Costs, Risks, and Benefits of Surgery. New York: Oxford University Press.

MURPHY, M. L., H. N. HULTGREN, K. DETRE, J. THOMSEN, T. TAKARO, et al. (1977a) "Treatment of chronic stable angina: A preliminary report of survival data of the randomized Veterans Administration Cooperative Study." N. Engl. J. Med. 297: 621-627.

——— (1977b) "Special correspondence." New England Journal of Medicine 197: 1470.

Office of Technology Assessment (1978) Assessing the Efficacy and Safety of Medical Technologies. Washington, DC: Government Printing Office.

PATON, B. C. (1978) "Who needs coronary bypass surgery?" Human Nature (September): 76-83.

PATTON, M. Q., P. S. GRIMES, K. M. GUTHRIE, N. J. BRENNAN, B. D. FRENCH, and D. A. BLYTH (1977) "In search of impact: an analysis of the federal health evaluation of programs, pp. 141-163 in C. H. Weiss (ed.) Using Social Research in Public Policy-Making. Lexington, MA: D. C. Heath.

PETO, R., M. C. PIKE, P. ARMITAGE, N. E. BRESLOW, D. R. COX, S. V. HOWARD, N. MANTEL, K. McPHERSON, J. PETO, and P. G. SMITH (1976) "Design and analysis of randomized clinical trials requiring prolonged observation of each patient: I. Introduction and design." British Journal of Cancer 34: 585-612.

PILLEMER, D. B. and R. J. LIGHT (1980) "Synthesizing outcomes: how to use research evidence from many studies." Harvard Educational Review 50: 176-195.

RENOU, P., A. CHANG, I. ANDERSON, and C. WOOD (1976) "Controlled trial of fetal intensive care." American Journal of Obstetrics and Gynecology 126: 470-476.

RIECKEN, H. W., R. F. BORUCH, D. T. CAMPBELL, N. CAPLAN, T. K. GLENNAN, J. W. PRATT, A. REES, and W. WILLIAMS (1974) Social Experimentation: A Method for Planning and Evaluating Social Intervention. New York: Academic.

RUFFIN, J. M., J. E. GRIZZLE, N. C. HIGHTOWER, G. McHARDY, H. SHULL, and J. B. KIRSNER (1969) "A co-operative double-blind evaluation of gastric 'freezing' in the treatment of duodenal ulcer." New England Journal of Medicine 281: 16-19.

SECHREST, L. and R. REDNER (forthcoming) "Strength and integrity of treatments in evaluation studies." Criminal Justice Evaluation Reports.

STAR, J. (1978) "The stricken heart: making it through the big event." Chicago (April): 124-133.

WAGNER, J. L. (1979) "Toward a research agenda on medical technology," in Medical Technology. NCHSR Research Proceedings Series, DHEW Publication (PHS) 79-3254. Washington, DC: Government Printing Office.

WANGENSTEEN, O. H., E. T. PETER, D. M. NICOLOFF, A. I. WALDER, H. SOSIN, and E. F. BERNSTEIN (1962) "Achieving 'physiological gastrectomy' by gastric freezing." Journal of the American Medical Association 180: 439-444.

WARNER, K. E. (1975) "A 'desperation-reaction' model of medical diffusion." Health Services Research 10: 369-383.

WEISS, C. H. (1977) "Introduction," in C. H. Weiss (ed.) Using Social Research in Public Policy-Making. Lexington, MA: D. C. Heath.

——— (1973) "Where politics and evaluation research meet." Evaluation 1, 3: 37-45.

William H. Yeaton
Lee Sechrest

University of Michigan

4

ESTIMATING EFFECT SIZE

We make important decisions each day of our lives. This is especially true in the health field, where decisions may have far-reaching effects on many people. We might overhear researchers and policy makers asking: "How effective is this new method of relieving pain? Is it too expensive to be readily accepted by the public? Does this treatment make a significant impact on the lives of its recipients? Are there any risks involved, and do the risks justify the benefits? How does this treatment compare with existing treatments for the same problem? Can doctors or patients easily adhere to the specifications of the treatment regimen? Will they notice differences in functioning? Which specific changes in functioning will we accept as valid criteria to reject or recommend this treatment?"

We share the discomfort the reader may experience when confronted by such questions. We have been woefully negligent in developing or even in recognizing the need for useful methods of estimating magnitudes of treatment effects. In a previous chapter (Sechrest and Yeaton, 1980), we rejected statistical

AUTHORS' NOTE: An earlier version of this chapter was presented at the Third Annual Meeting of the Evaluation Research Society, held in Minneapolis, October 18-20, 1979.

approaches to the problem of effect size estimation, principally because they rely so heavily on the specific features of the experimental design and its implementation. Meaningful generalizations to other experiments or real-life implementation are seriously questioned in these circumstances. The intent of this chapter is to offer alternative methods of assessing effectiveness of research pertinent to the health field but applicable to other fields as well. We do not pretend that these possibilities are faultless, but we do believe that they merit serious consideration and further study.

SIZE OF AN EXPERIMENTAL EFFECT

We encounter instances of experimental and quasi-experimental effects in the literature illustrated by these facsimiles: (a) The rate of utilization of services for the elderly was 17 percent higher among those with at least a high school education; (b) body temperature was one degree lower among children in the experimental group as contrasted to those in the control group; (c) the correlation between severity of presenting problem and treatment compliance was .56 for whites and .31 for blacks. These examples only describe results obtained from health studies; they do not interpret the findings. But interpretations are inevitable, and necessary, if we are to judge the importance of the work. And a judgment of effect size is critical both to any assessment of the significance of the results and to the credibility of the decisions regarding implementation of the findings.

The shortcomings of these examples are quite easy to pinpoint. None of them addresses the magnitude of effects produced. Knowing that utilization is 17 percent higher among a group of the better-educated elderly tells us nothing, literally, about the practical significance of this percentage differential. Is this difference a cause for elation? disappointment? How difficult (in terms of money and effort) is it to produce this difference? Analogously, is the one-degree reduction in body temperature found in the experimental group clinically significant? What if the reduction were three degrees? How risky is the treatment administered to obtain this difference? Finally, would the difference in relationship between severity of presenting problem and treatment compliance indicated in our third example represent some kind of bias among doctors? We cannot answer even one of these questions without some kind of quantitative measure of the size of the effect produced.

ANTICIPATING CHANGE: CONCEPTUAL ISSUES

It would be premature to present various methods for quantifying the magnitude of experimental effects without cautioning the reader to consider some of the features of research that may render statements concerning effect size inaccurate and misleading. We need to be informed about the conceptual relevance, strength, and integrity of a treatment in order to be confident about estimates of effect size. These three dimensions are fundamental and a prerequisite to any valid interpretation of an effect size estimate.

Conceptual Relevance of Treatment

Conceptual relevance of treatment refers to the extent to which a given treatment is appropriate to the problem at hand. It demands an understanding of the mechanism relating the causes and the problem, as well as the assumed manner by which the treatment will alleviate the problem. If underutilization of health services for the elderly is conceptualized as a deficiency in ability to read about available services in the newspaper due to relative lack of education, a treatment that broadcasts relevant information via radio is conceptually relevant. A treatment that delivers informational flyers to the doorsteps of the elderly is conceptually irrelevant, since the assumed link between knowledge of availability and tendency to utilize services is not modified; one's knowledge cannot be altered with unreadable information presented only in readable form. One of the writers (L.S.) knows of an instance in which an inexpensive protein food supplement was being advertised in newspapers when the target population was largely illiterate.

The importance of the conceptual relevance of treatment is illustrated cogently by the attempts of Alexander et al. (1979) to improve pulmonary functioning in children with asthma. Though flawed in various ways, previous work had suggested symptomatic benefits from brief relaxation training. The authors failed to replicate these benefits and used the possible conceptual irrelevance of relaxation to explain their results: It can be pointed out that the hypothesis may have been naive in the first place. . . . Physiological relaxation might even be considered to be counter-indicated in asthma (1979: 33). David Barlow (forthcoming) has criticized the frequent inclusion of relaxation training in packaged programs without testing the worth of this component: "From weight reduction to social skills training to insomnia and smoking, and in some cases even parenting books, relaxation is recommended as an important component." Obviously, the mechanism through which relaxation may mediate treatment effects is either not understood by researchers or not used as a basis on which to choose treatments.

Vaupel and Graham (1980) use conceptual relevance to criticize the United States' overreaction to the effects of a presumed overconsumption of eggs in our diets. While the cholesterol content in egg yolks is assumed to cause cardiovascular disease in humans, there are several links missing in this inferred causal chain. First, there appears to be no direct relationship between egg consumption and the amount of cholesterol in the blood. Further, high levels of cholesterol in blood plasma do not necessarily contribute to cardiovascular disease. The theory relating blood cholesterol levels and cardiovascular problems is suspect, given the poorly understood mechanisms mediating this inferred linkage. Without further study of the mediating factors involved, this and any other suggested causes of cardiovascular problems are likely to be conceptually irrelevant.

Strength of Treatment

Assuming that we are in a position of wanting to maximize treatment effectiveness, we would also choose a strong treatment as well as a conceptually relevant one. We must temper our judgments about magnitude of effect with our assessment of the strength of treatment administered. We should ordinarily not expect big effects with weak treatments. Discrepancies demand explanation. Strength of treatment refers to judgments of quantitative indicators available independently of outcome of the a priori likelihood that the treatment could have its intended effects. Strong treatments contain large amounts of whatever effective ingredients are involved. Our previously stated example, where conceptually relevant radio broadcasts were delivered to the elderly, would be considered strong to the extent that frequent, attention-demanding communications during prime radio time were involved. A rapid-smoking, aversive conditioning treatment involving frequent and deep inhalations over an extended period would be judged stronger than one involving infrequent and shallow inhalations for a brief duration. Though strength of treatment and effect size can vary independently, we contend that there is no way to divorce these two dimensions when assessing effectiveness. Sechrest and his colleagues (Sechrest and Redner, forthcoming; Sechrest et al., 1979) have elaborated strength-of-treatment issues elsewhere, and the interested reader is referred to these papers for a more detailed discussion.

Integrity of Treatment

Even when a conceptually relevant treatment is chosen to be administered in a strong form, it may not be delivered as planned. Integrity of treatment refers to the degree that the original treatment protocol is adhered to. If radio broadcasts to the elderly are delivered unenthusiastically for fewer minutes than planned, the integrity of treatment has lessened. Radio and television advertisers pay people to monitor their ads to make sure they are broadcast according to contract specifications. An evaluation of the effects of daycare and homemaker services to the chronically ill (Weissert et al., 1980) showing minimal beneficial changes must be tempered by the lack of documentation of actual service delivery. Mere attendance figures without data-based monitoring of services received by patients leaves open the possibility that minimal effectiveness is due to minimal delivery of services. We cannot say. But interpretation of the research findings is hampered considerably without documentation of the integrity of treatment. This we can say with assurance.

We maintain that the magnitude of effect demonstrated depends on all three of these dimensions. As conceptual relevance, strength, and integrity of treatment increase, so too should effect size. The precise nature of the functional relationship between each of these three dimensions and effect size is unknown to us. We would suppose the relationship to be monotonic, though perhaps the slope of the curve might well change at different dimension values. With some problem areas it might be most efficient to maximize integrity given an incompletely understood mechanism of change and a treatment expensive to administer in a strong form. With others, conceptual relevance might be the most important dimension to maximize. The possibility that effect size would vary with interactions among the three dimensions is quite plausible and researchable. That such questions have not yet been addressed empirically is easily attributable to researchers' and practitioners' desire to maximize treatment effectiveness. At the present time we must be extremely cautious to qualify our estimates of effect size with our knowledge of these three dimensions of treatment.

METHODS OF QUANTIFYING EFFECT SIZE

When we look at the statistics used to report research out-comes, the most obvious and usually the simplest piece of information is the probability or p value. That value gives an indication of the confidence we ought to have in the conclusion that there is an effect of the treatment (if the study involved an intervention). However, for reasons that are well known but, we think, often ignored, the p value provides almost no informa-tion about *how big* the effect is. If a decision maker is to spend money or human resources to produce the effect, or is to worry about it if it is undesirable, he or she must have additional information. Specifically, it is essential to know how big the effect is in some very practical sense. It is that practical sense that has so regularly been obscured by the hypnotic attraction of the test of significance (Meehl, 1978). Unfortunately, we lack any ready prescriptions for determining the size of effects obtained in research. As indicated earlier, we do not regard purely statistical approaches, such as proportion of variance accounted for, as being of much value (Sechrest and Yeaton, 1980). Consequently, we are working toward more empirical ways of accomplishing the goal.

Judgmental Approaches to Effect Size Estimation

Quite often, a subjective impression of the magnitude of experimental effects is made after viewing the results of re-search—a "looks big" or "looks small" approach to effect size estimation. Based on this subjective evaluation of size of effects, a policy decision is made to implement or abandon the treat-ment in other settings. To illustrate, a brief psychotherapeutic intervention designed to decrease high levels of seemingly un-warranted use of medical services has been described as reducing medical utilization by up to 75 percent over a five-year period. Offhand, that seems like a large (Cummings and Follette, 1976) and socially important effect. No statistical or other supplemental analyses are necessary to impress the reader. This simply looks like a big effect. In contrast, Freeborn and his associates (1978) found a 9.2 percent difference in utilization between groups exposed and not exposed to outreach workers' services. The difference is not obviously impressive, and the fact that it was shown to be statistically significant adds little.

These examples illustrate seemingly large and small effects. Should policy makers decide to implement the first and abandon the second treatment, their decisions may be correct more often than by chance or even by relying on statistical criteria. However, more intelligent decisions, ones that do not rely upon intuition alone, can be made. Or perhaps some persons will have better intuitions than others, a possibility to which we now turn.

Expert judgments. By virtue of their familiarity with a diverse range of treatment types and strength, experts may make accurate predictions of effect sizes. It is reasonable to assume that informed, subjective estimates would prove superior to those not based on any data. Experts may, then, be in a favored position to judge the magnitude of a particular effect, based on their knowledge of those previously found. To call an effect "miraculous" or "worthless" may only mean that it far exceeds or falls short of those previously produced. Experts in many fields are specially designated to judge the importance of change. In medicine, doctors must gauge changes in symptomatology to decide whether surgery is to be recommended. In this case, the magnitude estimation is of a threshold type where a binary decision is made—whether or not to operate.

A study by Emlet and his associates (1973) illustrates the use of experts to judge the magnitude of change. Judges were asked to estimate the benefits associated with various kinds of healthcare interventions for stroke victims. Results serve as a barometer of changes likely to be considered clinically significant. One could obtain such judgments in other health-related fields where special population, settings, and treatments are studied.

We have utilized experts to make a priori assessments of the strength of smoking treatments by estimating percentage of change expected. After reading capsulized descriptions of treatments published in the literature, experienced researchers and practitioners rated probable effects. These ratings were then correlated with actual study results. The average correlation was .47, and some judges achieved correlations in the .70s. Apparently, experts are reasonably accurate predictors of effect size even when relying only on written descriptions and not knowing treatment integrity.

We cannot disparage subjective judgments, since all decisions are subjective at some point in the decision-making process (even when one decides to rely on objective data). Attempts to remove the subjective element from the process—say, by accepting results as important when they are statistically significant and unimportant when they are statistically insignificant—are doomed to failure, since statistical significance depends on a variety of factors such as sample size and choice of control group as well as elements like strength, integrity, and conceptual relevance of treatment, noted earlier. We would prefer to make judgments "out front," opting for explicit criteria which can be critically scrutinized and improved.

Normative Approaches to Effect Size Estimation

The logic of the normative approach to magnitude estimation is quite simple. We commonly assess the size or importance of objects, events, or outcomes by comparison to some standard. In essence, we ask if something is bigger than or smaller than the average of similar somethings. A new treatment is better than previous ones if it has greater benefits and/or fewer risks. Similarly, an intervention that produces a greater change (effect) than most other interventions may be considered to have produced a large effect. If most efforts to reduce unnecessary utilization of medical services result in only a 5 to 10 percent reduction, an intervention that reduces utilization by, say 25 or 30 percent might seem impressive.

Treatment Effect Norms. We can construct norms by aggregating data from previous studies. For example, we can combine outcome measures in experiments previously completed, calculate a few, simple descriptive statistics, and evaluate a given treatment by comparing its results to those in the literature. Smith and Glass (1977) used this strategy to establish norms from a large number of therapy outcome studies. They reported a mean effect size of .68 standard deviation units' difference between experimental and control groups, and a standard deviation of that mean effect size of .67 units. We might regard a novel treatment with optimism if it exceeded the average effect size by more than one standard deviation, or be pessimistic about a treatment at, say, half a standard deviation below the mean. Jeffrey et al. (1978) used this normative approach to validate their weight-loss program, noting that the mean weight loss of 11.0 pounds reported in their study compared favorably with an average loss of 11.5 pounds found in 21 recent studies in the literature.

From a research bibliography on utilization of health services (Aday and Eichorn, 1972), we reviewed 37 studies reporting the correlates: age, education, income, occupation, race, location, SES, and sex. It was our intention to assess the relative and absolute contribution of these eight correlates to the use of various health practices. We wondered, for example, how much effect various income and educational levels had on the percentage of subjects utilizing services. Our basic unit of analysis was the largest difference reported in a specific study for a given correlate of utilization. For example, if subjects from four income levels showed 4 percent, 7 percent, 14 percent, and 11 percent use of available physicians, then the largest difference would be 10 percent (14-4 percent). With 533 such differences, we found that occupational and SES categories produced the largest utilization differences (21 percent and 20 percent, respectively), while sex and age produced the smallest differences (5 and 12 percent, respectively). These values, admittedly overestimates and imperfect, allow us to form rough expectations of the amount contributed by several correlates of utilization, to guess a likely order of contribution, and to speculate why some variables have greater impact than others, so that we may eventually make a more informed choice of which variables might be manipulted to maximize utilization.

We have reviewed 41 smoking-modification studies reporting percentage decrease in smoking as a dependent measure. An aggregation of data across different follow-up periods in these studies revealed a mean decrease in smoking of 53 percent ($\sigma = 27\%$) for experimental groups and 36 percent ($\sigma = 29\%$) for control groups. The large standard deviations indicate very discrepant findings, thus making any conclusions based on normative standards quite tentative. However, with these data in hand, an administrator of a community health center would be in a far better position to evaluate the merits of a novel approach to smoking modification. Should this new treatment produce six-month maintenance outcomes exceeding the large majority of interventions previously reported, a decision to implement the new program could be readily defended.

In principle, treatment effect norms can be established for any set of studies sharing the same dependent measure. In fact, it is only with considerable effort that such sets can be identified. The previously discussed smoking-modification studies illustrate the problem all too clearly. Results were typically reported as either percentage decrease in smoking or percentage of subjects who stopped smoking. The follow-up periods were not standardized, ranging from weekly to monthly reports. Moreover, outcome data were not always collected at the end of the treatment and not necessarily at the same time for both experimental and control groups. The situation with respect to standards of obtaining and reporting results of intervention studies is probably not better in other fields.

We would neither expect nor request complete standardization of methods of obtaining and reporting outcome data. We would, however, suggest the need for settling on at least a minimal degree of uniformity in reporting data. For example, smoking-modification studies might report percentage of subjects who stopped smoking at the end of treatment and at one-month, three-month, and six-month follow-up periods. Other measures and times of follow-up could supplement these minimal standards, at the discretion of authors. With this degree of standardization, large data sets with considerable homogeneity could be easily identified, thus allowing aggregation of subsets with similar treatments, subject populations, and settings. These subsets would contain a substantial number of cases, making possible comparison of different emergency medical interventions in similar cities or even the effects of a specific health insurance plan on different socioeconomic classifications throughout the United States.

Standards for Successful Treatment

For at least some treatments, it may be possible to define a standard by which treatment might be judged to have been successful, either in the individual case or across cases. For example, the standard for judging the effectiveness of one asthma treatment program that we are aware of is the ability of the patient to walk up ten flights of stairs. It seems to be fairly widely accepted that the standard for judging success of a cancer treatment is five-year survival. The Indian Health Service established standards for success in delivery of health services that included a maximum permissible rate of infant dehydration from gastroenteritis. Morphine is the standard by which analgesic potency is judged, and Alexander et al. (1979) set what they claimed to be the most commonly used symptomatic pharmacological treatment for asthma (nebulized isoproterenol hydrochloride) as the standard for judging other treatments. By their standard, then, relaxation training was judged to be relatively ineffective. In their study of homecare of the chronically ill, Weissert et al. (1980) included a group receiving both daycare and homemaker services, and the results in that group provided a standard by which to judge the effectiveness of either service given alone. In some ways, the setting of a standard for judging success is the opposite of judging success against the standard of no treatment at all. The advantage of the standard, however, is that it at least defines where one is in relation to some reasonable goal; merely to prove a treatment better than nothing may not be very revealing.

In a somewhat different approach to the problem of establishing measurement standards, Wilson (1978) has used the concept of microrisk (a risk which increases the chances of death by one in a million) as a kind of anchor or standard for comparison to existing or soon-to-be-initiated practices. He asserts that we demonstrate a willingness to accept the microrisks involved in such activities as drinking a half-liter of wine (cirrhosis of the liver) or eating 100 charcoal-broiled steaks (cancer caused by benzopyrene). Clearly, any single health practice which entails a microrisk of danger is likely to be accepted by consumers when there are noticeable benefits.

Normalization. The goal of most health interventions is to return the patient to a normal state of functioning. A physical therapist would probably cease treatment for the rehabilitation of atrophied muscles following a broken leg when muscle strength and size are comparable to those of the unbroken leg. In the same vein, an untreated control group or condition could serve as a standard against which to gauge an experimental effect. Ciarlo (1977) used precisely this logic by obtaining communitywide standards against which to compare the results of mental health interventions. The intent of the treatment was to alleviate a state of deficiency and not to produce self-actualized individuals. Moreover, treatment success was defined only as bringing persons within the general range of behavior usually accepted as "normal."

There are, however, many cases when normal control groups are inappropriate as adequate standards against which to measure treatment effects. Too many Americans smoke and drink; they also consume excess amounts of salt and sugar. To use Averagetown, U.S.A. as a barometer to assess lifestyle changes of at-risk patients would be woefully poor practice for either researchers or practitioners. It is precisely the normal practices of people that may need to be improved. A standard of health that is inherently deficient is just as inappropriate as one requiring superior effort to attain.

Standards and Magnitudes of Effects. It can be seen that the employment of standards fairly neatly sidesteps the issue of the magnitude of the intervention effect. Thus, with any given person or group, one might have to produce a small, or perhaps a very large, change in order to meet a standard. An antifebrile agent that "normalizes" low-grade fevers in a test group might or might not be clinically useful. On the other hand, a treatment which enables asthmatics to progress from climbing no stairs at all to climbing seven flights might have a fairly large effect, even if it does not bring many persons to the standard of ten flights. We think both the standards- and the magnitude-of-effect approaches to be of great value.

We noted also that even though achievement of a standard by a particular person may leave uncertain the question of magnitude of effect, the achievement of standards may in some cases be converted into a magnitude-of-effect measure by aggregating across cases. If several past treatments have averaged about 40 percent success in bringing persons up to some standard, and a new treatment brings 70 percent to standard, the magnitude of the treatment effect would be judged, normatively, to be rather large. That, after all, is about what is involved in judging success of antismoking programs, for which the standard of success is usually set at stopping altogether.

Absolute Values. Health interventions are often judged successful in terms of some absolute social value that is applied without respect to other aspects of a total intervention outcome. In our society, preservation of life is nearly an absolute value, and a given intervention may be judged to be important or even to have a large effect if it can be shown to save a life. Thus, for example, in an article about helicopter rescue and transport services (Potter, 1979), one authority was quoted to the effect that the cost of such services (perhaps $7000 per transport) are irrelevant in relation to their lifesaving value. Similarly, a burn center that avoids disfigurement or a community mental health center that can be shown to avert rape or child abuse may be thought to justify its existence in some absolute sense, even though the advantage gained in any comparative sense is small.

Despite the seductive appeal of reliance on absolute values, it possesses two primary shortcomings for the magnitude-of-effect problem. First, it may be extremely difficult to validate the saving of a life or the avoidance of an injury; the life "saved" or the injury "avoided" may simply be the fortuitous beneficiary of one treatment group. In Seattle, emergency medical units may claim a "save" by carefully documenting lifesaving efforts and receiving a favorable judgment from a committee empowered to make such decisions (Bergner, 1978). The second difficulty with the absolute-standard approach is the inevitable question of whether alternative strategies might lead to larger effects (e.g., more lives saved, more rapes averted) at the same expenditure of time and money, or to equal effects at a smaller expenditure. Society does not hesitate to spend thousands of dollars to save the life of a person now at risk; neither does it hesitate to demonstrate considerable caution in investing public funds for strategies likely to save the lives of unknown persons at unpredictable times. Even apparently absolute standard-of-effect size magnitude can be questioned in ways that qualify their absoluteness.

Costs and Benefits of Treatment

We place great value on a human life, but the value we place is finite. For example, we might be able to eradicate deaths on the highway at an exorbitant expense, by designing a system of vehicle transportation where impact between automobiles or between an automobile and a road hazard is impossible. We have not, and probably will not ever, design such a system. We would pay too heavy a price by foregoing certain other creature comforts—and place several occupations in jeopardy. Establishing dollar values for treatments and their outcomes is an extremely attractive practice, because dollars and cents are a common denominator for rating or ranking health practices and gauging the size of an experimental effect. With a financial accounting of costs, the decision rules become simple: Choose the least expensive program when outcomes are otherwise equal; choose the most effective program when costs are otherwise equal; and decide whether cost or effectiveness will have greater weight when programs are relatively more effective but cost more, or are relatively less effective but cost less.

Precedent teaches us that inexpensive solutions are important solutions, but initial solutions are seldom inexpensive. Dialysis machines were an extremely important treatment breakthrough for kidney disease, yet their current availability and impact are still largely due to government subsidy. We often applaud *any* treatment for a long-standing problem—albeit an expensive one such as a multimillion dollar cure for cancer (perhaps interferon from human blood)—since technology often develops a much less expensive version that achieves the same results. A relatively expensive development process exists for enhancing the quality of photographic negatives (Rose, 1980). The process would allow lower roentgen exposure during diagnostic X-rays, and therefore has tremendous implication for preventive health practice, *eventually*. The problem is reminiscent of Edison's quest to find an inexpensive yet durable filament for the incandescent electric light bulb that would replace platinum. Once the carbon filament was perfected, the electric bulb or "lamp," as it was then called, was cheap enough to make the gas light obsolete.

Decision-Making. Informed policy decisions demand a complete elaboration of the costs of an intervention, an intention not easily followed in practice. To illustrate, suppose we could increase compliance to a drug regimen by simply asking a physician to request an explicit statement of commitment from each patient to take a drug as prescribed. Any amount of increase in compliance would probably be viewed as worthwhile since there is little apparent cost in producing the beneficial change. However, the cost of educating physicians to request and obtain such statements is not likely to be trivial. It may be extremely difficult to estimate the (presumed) psychological

cost of receiving a painful shot, even when the potential benefits are obvious.

Economists use yet another concept, opportunity cost, to
refer to the cost of foregoing another alternative. For example,
the funds invested in coronary-artery bypass surgery may reduce the opportunity to invest in research on an artificial heart.
By whatever means, actuarial, psychological, or economic, the
identification of explicit or implicit costs of treatment is often a
difficult task.

To determine whether the costs of treatment exceed its
benefits we must be able to estimate the dollar value of benefits. The problem is more easily stated than solved. For example, if the intent of a program is to save lives, we establish
limits on the amount we are willing to pay, and therefore on the
value we place on a life. Cobb and Alvarez (n.d.) estimate that
Seattle's Mobile Cardiac Care Units cost approximately $3500
to save a single life. A decision to terminate this program means,
in blatantly frank terms, that we would not pay more than
$3500 to save the life of a person known only stochastically.
Implied dollar values of injuries avoided, rapes prevented, or
child abuse averted could be determined analagously.

Although we may wish to estimate the dollar value of lives
saved (but see Rhoads, 1978; Wilson, 1975), choice among
alternative programs does not necessitate this calculation. We
can choose that emergency intervention saving the most lives at
the least cost, for instance. When dependent measures are the
same, we need only know the cost for each unit of benefit.
These so-called proxy measures combined with costs of treatment become sufficient standards for comparing the effectiveness of treatment.

From a decision maker's vantage point, cost of treatment and
outcomes is only one of the many perspectives that assist in
quantifying the worth of a program. The expected magnitude of
political effect (the number of votes produced) and the ethical
implications of a health intervention, regardless of either cost or
effectiveness, are critical factors in its potential acceptability.
Weisbrod (1968) notes that relatively low benefit-cost ratios are

no assurance that programs will be adopted before those with higher ratios. Why? We might speculate that the benefits may be distributed inequitably to uncertain segments of society (e.g., rich and poor) or that the values of our culture clash with aspects of a program (e.g., free birth control for teenagers).

The complications of this magnitude-of-effect approach, already enormous, are further compounded by our inability to predict costs and benefits. Haynes and his associates (1978) found increased absenteeism to be associated with detection and labeling of hypertensive patients, an undesirable though unanticipated outcome with clear cost implications to an employer. Neill et al. (1978) found a high incidence of marital discord between spouses when one member had undergone intestinal bypass surgery. Not only is the finding unanticipated, but also we would face considerable difficulty categorizing the result, should the discord lead to a divorce. Would we count divorce as an unexpected benefit (to the seeker of the divorce) or as an unintended cost (to the recipient of the request for divorce)? The imperfections of the approach are clearly as obvious as its potential.

Quantification of Risk. Risk analysis is intimately related to cost and benefit analysis, since dollar values can be computed for risks incurred or avoided. For example, Wilson (1979a) suggests that cigarette companies pay a tax of 70 cents per cigarette to balance the increased cost to society from fire hazards, reduced working time, and hospital costs. Insurance companies protect us from various automobile, house, and hospital hazards, and we pay considerably for the benefit of this reduced risk. So, to the extent that we applaud cost and benefit analyses as important features on which to base decisions, risk analysis also offers an attractive standard of comparison of different programs.

Health is an area of inquiry particularly pertinent to the concept of risk. We must decide whether to birth our children in the hospital or at home, and our subjective assessment of the risk incurred in both settings may critically affect our decisions. A more informed decision could be made if we had normative data showing the risks of various kinds of complications given certain characteristics of the parents (e.g., previous pregnancy problems, physical condition of mother). Similarly, a patient might decide, quite rationally, not to be placed in an intensive care unit if the risks avoided were so slight that the extra financial cost outweighed the combination of increased risk and decreased cost of not entering. Diagnostic X-rays for breast cancer are valuable when the benefit of X-rays (decreased risk of breast cancer) exceeds the cost of not having X-rays (increased risk of undetected breast cancer). There is some evidence (Acosta et al., 1980) that a relatively simple visual field examination, though less expensive and generally less accurate than a CT scan or a cerebral angiogram, is the preferred diagnostic tool for certain opthamologic problems given the increased risk suffered from the CT scan and the cerebral angiogram.

In all the examples in the preceding paragraph, the concept of risk is integral to a valid decision about health practice. And the accuracy of the risk estimate relies on the morbidity and mortality rates calculated from normative standards. Wilson (1979b) estimates the risk of an increased likelihood of cancer by comparing actuarial data of humans exposed to cigarette smoking and radiation with otherwise comparable groups not exposed. However, such norms must be constantly updated to reflect changes in exposure rates and levels of exposure as public awareness of risk generates safer health practices. Some data by Gori and Lynch (1978) illustrate this point nicely, as pre-1960 cigarettes contained significantly more cigarette smoke constituents (e.g., tar, nicotine) than do modern versions. The risk in smoking a pack of pre-1960 cigarettes would be considerably more than the risk in smoking a pack of the same brand today, and this decreased risk should be reflected in decreased mortality. But given the fact that the results of today's consumption may only become apparent after a considerable time lag, we will always be confronted with outdated risk data when there is a delay in the cause-effect relationship.

The foregoing discussion of "safer" cigarettes brings to light an assumption implicit in this analysis of risk. We have assumed that people will choose to reduce risk where possible. However, knowing that each cigarette smoked potentially subtracts five minutes from one's life (Wilson, 1979a) is not likely to cause people to stop smoking. Furthermore, people who stop smoking may act to equalize their risk by drinking more heavily. This is akin to drivers wearing their seatbelts—and increasing their average speed. Conversely, could we expect some safer health practice to follow initiation of a riskier practice? Do individuals possess a kind of risk set point? The answers to questions such as these have critical implications for any researcher who claims that a large risk reduction should be translated as a large magnitude of effect.

DEMONSTRATING CHANGE: CONCEPTUAL ISSUES

The suggestions we have proposed for measuring the importance and magnitude of an experimental effect may have focused attention away from issues that influence a valid evaluation of effect size. These conceptual issues act as qualifiers to any implication that effect size estimation can be made to follow rigid guidelines. In the final section of this chapter we will elaborate on some of the dimensions of effect size which argue against the case that size alone determines effectiveness.

Multiple Outcome Measures

Good experimental practice dictates that we obtain several dependent measures of change. Accordingly, a researcher may measure physiological, written, and verbal behavior, calculate valid effect size estimators, and be embarrassed to find that the three measures do not agree in the extent of change produced. This perplexing result may be explained, justified, or even rationalized by the author, but it is not a comfortable position to find oneself in. Here is an instance where consistent, albeit small, effects would be welcomed as stronger evidence of change. Inconsistency demands explanation.

The situation is quite different when a researcher can predict the pattern of change using established theory, for then the inconsistency of effect size may actually enhance the believability of findings. Alexander et al. (1979) selected twelve lung-volume and pulmonary measures in their study of the effects of relaxation training on asthmatic children. The fact that only the two effort-dependent measures showed weak evidence of beneficial change while the other ten variables remained essentially unchanged substantiates their conclusion that relaxation is an ineffective treatment for asthma.

Worthwhile Small Effects

Seemingly small effects may in some instances alter an existing course of events to produce an ultimately large change. We term such a change a "nudge" effect, noting that the nudge can produce beneficial or detrimental results. A heartrending plea from a child has been known to cause a parent to verbalize a commitment to stop smoking. Perhaps there may have been an existing motivation to change so that a small but appropriately timed nudge set into motion a lifetime of abstention. Early educational efforts to produce long-standing dental hygiene habits are probably of the nudge variety. Preventive programs are based partly on this logic. On the other hand, early initiation into the joys of sugar may occasion a lifelong "sweet tooth." It may only take one drink to reestablish a converted alcoholic.

We should cherish beneficial nudges when we find them, since they are so thrifty of effort and expense. Unfortunately, it is difficult to discriminate a genuine nudge from a merely small effect. The best that we can suggest is a careful study of effects that have proved to be of the nudge variety, from which some characteristics of nudges and problem types can be established.

There is another case where effect size may be minimal at first glance, but substantial when analyzed more carefully. Small individual effects can be greatly magnified when aggregated across a large number of units. A small percentage increase in the tendency of individuals to utilize self-care techniques for minor problems would have a tremendous impact nationwise (Olbrisch, 1979). Huge sums of money for organizations such as the March of Dimes have been raised by encouraging each individual to contribute pocket change. A weight loss of ten pounds in one year would follow from reduction of food intake by 100 calories each day. Laws that prohibit smoking in public places not only eliminate the small but cumulatively deleterious effects of secondhand smoke, but also can amount to many, many cigarettes over a lifetime (if we can assume that smokers do not smoke more at permissible times). When researchers produce small effects that can be persuasively argued to aggregate across individuals or time, the magnitude of change, viewed at this level of analysis, is conspicuously increased.

Qualitative Dimensions of Change

There are qualitative dimensions to change that we must not ignore in our use of effect size indicators. We often view the years saved in avoidance of highway deaths from the high-incidence group of young drivers, for example, to be of a higher quality than the years saved through early diagnosis of cancer in 50-year-olds.

We have previously maintained that small may indeed be beautiful if important change can be attributed either to desirable nudges or to accumulated small benefits. Analogously, big may be ugly unless substantial change is reflected in qualitative differences. A 25-pound weight loss by an obese person may be meaningless in terms of enhanced self-esteem unless a spouse, friends, or acquaintances notice the difference and react in a way likely to sustain the change and spur subsequent weight reduction. One might look with disdain on the finding (Weinstein et al., 1977) showing that the coronary bypass operation does not extend life expectancy unless one also realizes that quality of life is improved during the survival time. In the first instance a seemingly large change is trivial, and in the second instance an apparently small change is important when a qualitative indicator of change supplements a quantitative measure of effect size.

The argument we have presented for substantiating quantitative change with qualitative measures can also be applied in reverse. We should also validate subjective measures of change with their behavioral implications. Subjective ratings of diminished severity of migraine headaches attributable to treatment (e.g., Lake et al., 1979) would be considerably strengthened by performance measures of change. Can we expect greater efficiency and output at home and on the job when the mean daily headache rating improves by .1 or .5? In the same way that aerobic points are validated by consumption of oxygen and the cardiovascular benefit of the exercise (Cooper, 1970), rating scale points could and should be validated via implications in the actual performance of each individual.

Perception of Change

A treatment can produce a dramatic change in behavior, possibly bigger than any change ever produced, yet not be perceived to be of meaningful magnitude, even when the data are of high quality. Program participants may also believe that desirable outcomes have occurred when none has been demonstrated. We have discussed this troublesome result elsewhere (Sechrest and Yeaton, forthcoming), providing examples and a model for understanding this apparent anomaly. Perhaps the imperfect relationship between change and perceived change can be understood by examining the pattern of change. Immediate yet transient effects may yield statements of change when the analysis reports no (substantial or statistically significant) differences. It is also possible that change is "felt" by subjects but goes unmeasured by researchers, as when placebos produce "hidden" physiological effects. A treatment that induces gradual change may, on the other hand, be imperceivable. To study strength, integrity, and conceptual relevance of treatment but to ignore the difference between effects and perceived effects would leave a monumental void in a comprehensive study of effect size magnitudes.

CONCLUSION

What we have asked, simply put, is, "How can one determine whether the impact of a treatment is important?" Unfortunately, simple questions do not necessarily generate simple answers.

We have argued that researchers must temper any estimations of the magnitude of effects demonstrated with an accurate assessment of the strength, integrity, and conceptual relevance of treatment. Matters are further complicated by the realization that results cannot be classified or measured in rigid, absolute ways. For instance, "small" effects may be deceptively worthwhile, while apparently large effects may make a trivial difference in the quality of a participant's life. However, we suggest that an effect is important to the extent that a designated expert judges it to be so, or when it compares favorably to previously reported effects. In some cases, a researcher can take advantage of existing standards to evaluate the importance of results. Moreover, the possibility of expressing costs, benefits, and risks of treatments and effects in readily comparable terms like dollars and probabilities should not be ignored. Until the matter of effect size is well understood and good estimates can be made, decision makers in health care, as in other fields, will not be in a position to take full advantage of research findings known to them.

REFERENCES

ACOSTA, P. C., J. D. TROBE, J. SHUSTER, and J. KRISCHER (1980) "Visual fields in the management of unexplained visual loss: a cost-benefit analysis." (unpublished)

ADAY, L. A. and R. L. EICHORN (1972) "The utilization of health services: indices and correlates: a research bibliography." DHEW Publication (HSM) 73-3003. Washington, DC: Government Printing Office.

ALEXANDER, A. B., G.J.A. CROPP, and H. CHAI (1979) "Effects of relaxation training on pulmonary mechanics in children with asthma." Journal of Applied Behavior Analysis 12: 27-35.

BARLOW, D. H. (forthcoming) "Behavior therapy: the next decade." Behavior Therapy.

BERGNER, L. (1978) Personal communication.

CIARLO, J. A. (1977) "Monitoring and analysis of mental health program outcome data." Evaluation 4: 109-114.

COBB, L. A. and H. ALVAREZ (n.d.) "III Medic I: the Seattle system for management of out-of-hospital emergencies." University of Washington and Harborview Medical Center. (unpublished)

COOPER, K. H. (1970) The New Aerobics. New York: Bantam.

CUMMINGS, N. A. and W. T. FOLLETTE (1976) "Brief psychotherapy and medical utilization," in The Professional Psychologist Today. San Francisco: Jossey-Bass.

EMLET, H. E., J. W. WILLIAMSON, D. L. DITTMER, and J. L. DAVIS (1973) Estimated Health Benefits and Costs of Post-Onset Care of Stroke. Baltimore: Johns Hopkins University.

FREEBORN, D. K., J. P. MULLOOLY, T. COLOMBO, and V. BURNHAM (1978) "The effect of outreach workers' services on the medical care utilization of a disadvantaged population." Journal of Community Health 3: 306-320.

GORI, G. B. and C. J. LYNCH (1978) "Towards less hazardous cigarettes: current advances." Journal of the American Medical Association 240: 1255-1259.

HAYNES, R. B., D. L. SACKETT, D. W. TAYLOR, E. S. GIBSON, and A. L. JOHNSON (1978) "Increased absenteeism from work after detection and labeling of hypertensive patients." New England Journal of Medicine 299: 741-744.

JEFFREY, R. W., R. R. WING, and A. J. STUNKARD (1978) "Behavioral treatment of obesity: the state of the art, 1976." Behavior Therapy 9: 189 199.

LAKE, A., J. RAINEY, and J. D. PAPSDORF (1979) "Biofeedback and rational-emotive therapy in the management of migraine headache." Journal of Applied Behavior Analysis 12: 127-140.

MEEHL, P. E. (1978) "Theoretical risks and tabular asterisks: Sir Karl, Sir Ronald, and the slow progress of soft psychology." Journal of Consulting and Clinical Psychology 46: 806-834.

NEILL, J. R., J. R. MARSHALL, and C. E. YALE (1978) "Marital changes after intestinal bypass surgery." Journal of the American Medical Association 240: 447-450.

OLBRISCH, M. E. (1979) "Evaluation of a stress management program for high utilizers of a prepaid university health service." Ph.D. dissertation, Florida State University, Tallahassee.

POTTER, J. (1979) "Aviation units: are they worth the money?" Police Magazine (July): 20-25.

RHOADS, S. E. (1978) "How much should we spend to save a life?" Public Interest 51: 74-92.

ROSE, K. J. (1980) "Reducing the X-ray hazard." Omni (April): 35.

SECHREST, L. and R. REDNER (forthcoming) "Strength and integrity of treatments in evaluation studies." Criminal Justice Evaluation Reports.

SECHREST, L. and W. H. YEATON (forthcoming) "Empirical bases for estimating effect size," in R. F. Boruch et al. (eds.) Secondary Analysis in Applied Social Research.

――― (1980) "Estimating magnitudes of experimental effects." (unpublished)

SECHREST, L., S. G. WEST, M. A. PHILLIPS, R. REDNER, and W. H. YEATON (1979) "Some neglected problems in evaluation research: strength and integrity of treatments," in L. Sechrest et al., Evaluation Studies Review Annual, Volume 4. Beverly Hills, CA: Sage.

SMITH, M. L. and G. V. GLASS (1977) "Meta-analysis of psychotherapy outcome studies." American Psychologist 32: 752-760.

VAUPEL, J. W. and J. D. GRAHAM (1980) "Egg in your bier?" Public Interest 58: 3-17.

WEINSTEIN, M. C., J. S. PLISKIN, and W. B. STASON (1977) "Coronary artery bypass surgery: decision and policy analysis," in J. P. Bunker et al. (eds.) Costs, Risks, and Benefits of Surgery. New York: Oxford University Press.

WEISBROD, B. A. (1968) "Income redistribution effects and benefit-cost analysis," in S. S. Chase, Jr. (ed.) Problems in Public Expenditure Analysis. Washington, DC: Brookings Institute.

WEISSERT, W. G., T.T.H. WAN, and B. B. LIVIERATOS (1980) Effects and Costs of Day Care and Homemaker Services for the Chronically Ill: A Randomized Experiment. DHEW Publication (PHS) 79-3258. Springfield, VA: National Technical Information Service.

WILSON, R. (1979a) "Analyzing the daily risks of life." Technology Review (February): 41-46.

――― (1979b) "Quantitative estimates of carcinogenic risk." Harvard University. (unpublished)

――― (1978) "The concept of risk." CTFA Cosmetic Journal 10: 22-27.

――― (1975) "Examples in risk-benefit analysis." Chemical Technology 6: 604-607.

5

James L. Rogers
Olga M. Haring
John P. Goetz

Northwestern University

TRACER METHODOLOGY

The rapid expansion of medical technology that presently is occurring has frequently not been accompanied by documented benefits to the patient. This is true of computer-automated medical record systems, commonly referred to as Medical Information Systems (MIS). In this chapter, a methodological approach normally used to evaluate the quality of care in clinical settings, called the "tracer methodology," is used in a modified form to assess the direct impact of MIS technology on the process and outcome of health care.

MIS technology has been developed for a variety of medical settings and technical descriptions of several systems are available (Beilin et al., 1974; Bradshaw-Smith, 1976; Cobelli and Salvan, 1975; Grossman et al., 1973; Kennedy et al., 1968; McDonald et al., 1977; Mellner et al., 1976; NCHSR, 1976; Schenthal et al., 1963; Schmidt et al., 1974; Slack et al., 1966;

AUTHORS' NOTE: This chapter is based on a paper presented at the Third Annual Meeting of the Evaluation Research Society held in Minneapolis, October 18-20, 1979. The major support for this project was provided by Grant HS 02649 from the National Center for Health Services Research, HRA. Initial data collection and analysis were made possible by DHEW Grant H500674 and USPHS Grant RR 05370 (NIH).

Wiekham et al., 1975). However, as a recent Office of Technology assessment report on MIS notes, "few careful evaluative studies have been conducted to date" (Ehrenhaft et al., 1977). Although evaluations which are available usually have not randomly created experimental and control groups, initial data from uncontrolled studies are promising. Current reports suggest that MISs are accepted by physicians, improve access to information, facilitate patient management and research, and provide educational opportunities (Battele Columbus Laboratories, 1976; Bulpitt et al., 1976; Ehrenhaft et al., 1977; Grossman et al., 1973; McDonald, 1976b; McDonald et al., 1977; Mellner et al., 1976; Schmidt et al., 1974; Starfield et al., 1977).

Although the above evaluative areas are important, they do not address the fundamental issue of whether MIS will directly influence patients by improving the process and outcome of health care. Perhaps this is true because understanding the direct impact of MIS technology on patients involves a methodological complication. Not all patients have the same problems, and each patient may have more than one problem. Thus, it is difficult to determine whether or not adequate care is being given by collecting data across patients at a given point in time, a difficulty very familiar to those evaluating the quality of care in clinical settings (i.e., peer review). In the case of peer review, the usual evaluative technique is an implicit review of the patient-physician interaction by a panel that periodically examines the medical record (Novick et al., 1976). This procedure, however, has been criticized as lacking standardization and being arbitrary and costly in physician time (Williamson, 1971).

Kessner et al. (1973) have suggested an alternative to implicit peer review which is called the "tracer methodology." This procedure examines patient care over an episode of illness rather than events occurring during a given patient visit. In its original conception, the tracer methodology calls for the selection of patients with a given medical problem and the subsequent examination of medical procedures they receive to determine whether predetermined treatment criteria are being met. The tracer method does not attempt to ascertain whether all medical problems for a given patient are being adequately treated, as is usually the case in implicit peer review, but whether in a given environment adequate treatment is being administered for a specific problem. The "tracer diseases" that are evaluated, of course, are of major concern to a particular setting; but in the truest sense, they are but a sample of the medical problems that exist.

A distinct advantage of the tracer methodology is that data collection can be carried out by paramedical abstractors who review the medical chart. Novick et al. (1976) compared the results of an assessment of clinical care obtained by the tracer method with results from an implicit review by a panel of physicians. Although these investigators report statistically significant correlations between results obtained by these methods, the tracer methodology avoided the "most time-consuming aspect of the study . . . [the] satisfactory involvement of the implicit reviewers, all of whom had busy schedules of teaching and patient care activities." A further benefit of the tracer methodology was that specific remedial deficiencies in health-care service were pinpointed, in contrast to the global, highly subjective statements which sometimes result from implicit peer review. These deficiencies per se could be passed on to attending physicians. Overall, the tracer methodology would seem to be comparable, if not preferable, to implicit peer review.

Clearly, the problems involved in assessing the impact of MIS technology on the direct care and outcome of patients substantially overlap with those of peer review. In both instances, the essential goal is to determine what actually occurs during, and results as a consequence of, the patient-physician interaction. This similarity in purpose underscores the present use of the tracer methodology to evaluate the impact of MIS technology on patient care. Two disease areas, diabetes and coronary disease, have been selected to study the impact of the Northwestern University Computerized Medical Record Summary System on health care in several specialty clinics.

Because the tracer methodology was originally intended for peer review, not technological impact assessment, some modifications in the usual procedure were necessary. First, groups were randomly created, one using the MIS (the experimental group) and the other using a manual, source-oriented medical record (the control group). Thus, the comparison of interest in this study is between these two conditions rather than between the medical care received by patients and predetermined criteria of care. Our randomized design allows the detection of the difference that MIS technology makes relative to what occurs in the absence of MIS; we do not wish to enter the "criteria" controversy and therefore have not compared medical care received in either condition to other reference criteria. It is readily acknowledged that MIS technology could possibly move medical care in a positive direction, with care still falling short of the ideal. In this chapter the direction of movement is the predominant issue.

A second modification of the original conception of the tracer methodology is the measurement of outcome of care as well as process of care. Outcome measures provide a "bottom line" assessment of the impact of any existing or new medically related procedure and, from an evaluation point of view, make a priori criteria of care for a given health-care episode a less essential feature of an evaluation plan (Lebow, 1974).

In summary, then, this study focuses on two tracer diseases, comparing randomly created experimental and control conditions on various aspects of process of care and parameters of outcome of care that are widely accepted as appropriate to each disease. Our emphasis is on the relative differences between conditions on these measurements that result due to the use of MIS, not on the compliance of these measurements with an a priori definition of good care.

PROCEDURES

The present report concerns one phase of a larger evaluation of the Northwestern University Computerized Medical Record Summary System, an MIS designed for use in the University's Cardiac, Pulmonary and Renal (CPR) specialty clinics. Beyond variables reflecting hospitalization patterns, general health, patient perceptions, and patient attitudes, specific data were collected to examine the process and outcome of care in six tracer disease areas: organic heart disease, pulmonary disease, diabetes, hypertension, obesity, and renal disease. This chapter reports the findings for diabetes and organic heart disease, while the remaining tracer areas will be subsequently reported.

A complete description of this MIS is available elsewhere (Greenburg et al., 1971; Haring, 1973; Haring et al., 1974), but a brief description is in order here. The system generates an eight-page summary for each patient visit. It provides the clinician with a concise and legible summary of the patient's record, identifies clinicians' recommendations (i.e., tests or procedures ordered) that were not carried out, flags omissions in the recording of observations and in the recording of recommended treatment, detects deficiencies in medical reasoning, recommends corrective actions, and provides ongoing educational opportunities for physicians and students. The summary includes a problem list, vital signs, cardiac-pulmonary-renal diagnoses, treatments, routine and specialized laboratory tests, and suggestions to the physician concerning patient care.

Approximately 1200 patients met the following criteria for inclusion in the study: (a) Patients must have attended the CPR clinics for at least six months prior to selection; (b) patients regularly receiving treatment in the psychiatric clinic were to be excluded, since there might be a reason that the patient might attend irregularly; and (c) female patients with pregnancies were to be excluded from the study, since this might have a confounding effect on their care within the CPR clinics. Of these, 484 patients were randomly selected and each was in turn randomly assigned to either the experimental condition that used the MIS or the control condition that used the traditional, source-oriented medical record. Five patients withdrew from the clinics before the study began, leaving 241 experimental and 238 control patients.

Groups of approximately 80 experimental and 80 control patients were phased into the study at different starting times. Clinic physicians were randomly assigned to either experimental or control patients, as well as to a third category where physicians saw patients from either condition in order to accommodate various scheduling problems (e.g., unscheduled patient visits). All clinic personnel, including physicians, were told only that an MIS was being phased into use, thus drawing attention away from the experiment per se. At the end of each of two consecutive years in the study, trained paramedic personnel retrospectively reviewed the patients' records. Data were recorded on a standardized evaluation form and then entered into a computerized data base.

In the following section, experimental patients will be compared to control patients on parameters that reflect the process and outcome of care for the conditions of diabetes and organic heart disease. Process-of-care parameters include the incidence of the following examinations and procedures: test for blood sugar, assignment/review of diet, examination of blood urea nitrogen or creatinine, funduscopic examination, examination of potassium and the examination of serum lipids or triglycerides. These are laboratory procedures often considered crucial to the continuity of care in the two disease areas considered here. Their selection was based on a consideration of published medical criteria as well as discussion with university physicians. Outcome-of-care parameters include blood sugar level, presence of glycosuria, electrocardiogram status, presence of heart-related defects, and blood pressure.

RESULTS

Results for the data analysis are reported in what follows, first for patients with diabetes and second for patients with organic heart disease. These disease areas will be reviewed separately, each section containing a description of baseline similarities and differences between the two conditions, a report of findings for the process-of-care parameters and, last, a report of findings on outcome of care. For convenience, baseline data are collectively presented for both disease areas in Tables 5.1 and 5.2. Process- and outcome-of-care data are presented separately for each disease area in Tables 5.3 and 5.4.

TABLE 5.1 Baseline Characteristics for Experimental and Control Patients

	Diabetes		Organic Heart Disease	
	Experimental (N = 80)	Control (N = 51)	Experimental (N = 166)	Control (N = 170)
Age (mean)	59.9 ± 2.5[a]	63.7 ± 2.5	58.1 ± 2.2	58.5 ± 2.3
Sex				
male	38 (47.5)[b]	19 (37.3)	74 (44.6)	61 (35.9)
female	42 (52.5)	32 (62.7)	92 (55.4)	109 (64.1)
Race				
black	43 (53.8)[c]	23 (45.1)	91 (54.8)[d]	83 (48.8)
white	32 (40.0)	28 (54.9)	70 (42.2)	83 (48.8)
other	4 (5.0)	0 (0.0)	3 (1.8)	4 (2.4)
Fee schedule				
public aid	39 (48.7)	21 (41.2)	74 (44.6)	62 (36.5)
minimal fee	0 (00.0)	0 (0.0)	1 (0.6)	1 (0.6)
1/3 fee	20 (25.0)	21 (41.2)	38 (22.9)	57 (33.5)
1/2 fee	7 (8.8)	2 (3.9)	10 (6.0)	12 (7.1)
2/3 fee	13 (16.3)	4 (7.8)	37 (22.3)	21 (12.4)
other	1 (1.2)	3 (5.9)	6 (3.6)	16 (9.4)
Prior CPR Attendance (mean months)	73.5 ± 11.7	99.6 ± 19.2	87.3 ± 9.9	109.0 ± 12.5
CPR chart weight (mean ounces)	22.9 ± 2.3	28.6 ± 4.6	24.1 ± 2.0	27.1 ± 2.3

a. 95% confidence intervals reported with means
b. percentages in parenthesis
c. one missing observation
d. two missing observations

Diabetes

There were 131 patients diagnosed as diabetic in the study—80 experimental and 51 control patients. By the end of the second year of the study, 92 patients were still attending the CPR clinics. Of the experimental patients, 4 had died, while 20 patients had transferred to other clinics, moved, or left for unknown reasons. The control group had one and 15 patients(s) in these respective categories, a distributional difference not significantly different from the experimental group (p > .05).

Even though patients were randomly assigned to either the experimental or control group, differences on baseline parameters could occur by chance. Therefore, several baseline characteristics for patients with diabetes are available in Tables 5.1 and 5.2. The incidence of hypertension, renal disease, obesity, pulmonary disease, and organic heart disease, and the total number of these diseases present, did not differ greatly between the experimental and control groups. Also, differences between the two groups in racial distribution and sex were not large. Relatively large chance differences were found to exist between the groups for fee schedule distribution, age, CPR medical chart weight, and prior CPR attendance. When these baseline differences were incorporated into the analysis of process- and outcome-of-care measures, no substantive change in results occurred. Consequently, the following process and outcome data have not been broken down along any baseline dimensions in order to simplify the presentation.

Process of Care. Two indices for the process of care were selected—frequency of examination of blood sugar (FBS, two-hour PCS, or GTT) during the two-year period, and the number of diets given or reviewed during the second year. (The latter item was not available to us for the first year of the study.)

The patients were classified according to whether a blood sugar test was administered during the first year only, the second year only, both years, or neither year. The number of experimental patients in each of these categories, respectively, was 11 (13.7 percent), 2 (2.5 percent), 46 (57.5 percent), and

TABLE 5.2 Baseline Incidence of Six Common Diseases Found in the patient Population

Other Diseases Present	Patients with Diabetes		Patients with Organic Heart Disease	
	Experimental (N = 80)	Control (N = 51)	Experimental (N = 166)	Control (N = 170)
Hypertension	64 (80.0)[a]	43 (84.3)	120 (72.3)[b]	111 (65.3)[b]
Renal disease	18 (22.5)	11 (21.6)	30 (18.1)	18 (10.6)
Obesity	49 (61.2)	31 (60.8)	73 (44.0)	64 (37.6)
Diabetes	—	—	55 (33.1)	39 (22.9)
Pulmonary disease	22 (27.5)[b]	9 (17.6)	35 (21.1)[c]	33 (19.4)
Organic heart disease	59 (73.7)	40 (78.4)	—	—
Number of Other Diseases present				
None	0 (0.0)	0 (0.0)	17 (10.2)	34 (20.0)
One disease	8 (10.0)	4 (7.8)	48 (28.9)	49 (28.8)
Two diseases	24 (30.0)	15 (29.4)	50 (30.1)	49 (28.8)
Three diseases	37 (46.2)	28 (54.9)	40 (24.1)	34 (20.0)
Four diseases	10 (12.5)	4 (7.8)	10 (6.0)	4 (2.4)
Five diseases	1 (1.2)	0 (0.0)	1 (0.6)	0 (0.0)

a. percentages in parenthesis
b. one observation missing
c. two observations missing

95

21 (26.2 percent). Corresponding figures for the control group are 11 (21.6 percent), 3 (5.9 percent), 28 (54.9 percent), and 9 (17.6 percent). The distribution did not differ significantly between experimental and control patients (X^2 [3] = 3.1, p > .05). Of the 67 experimental and 44 control patients seen during the second year, 24 (35.8 percent) of the experimental patients and 22 (50.0 percent) of the control patients had a diet given or reviewed. Again, there was no statistically significant difference between the experimental and control conditions (X^2 [1] = 2.2, p = .14), though more experimental patients had diets than did control patients (64.2 percent versus 50.0 percent).

Outcome of Care. Two measures of outcome for diabetic patients were selected—the blood sugar level and the presence of glycosuria. The mean blood sugar level for experimental patients at the beginning of the study was 151.5 mg./dl. (N = 34, SD = 61.3), with control patients having a mean of 156.9 mg./dl. (N = 17, SD = 62.2), a difference not statistically significant (p > .05). At the end of the two-year period, the means for the experimental and control groups were 144.4 mg./dl. (N = 29, SD = 49.6) and 134.4 mg./dl. (N = 18, SD = 39.0) respectively; again, the difference was not statistically significant (p > .05).

A classification of glycosuria present, glycosuria not present, or no information available was made for each patient at the beginning and end of both the first and second years of the study. The incidence of glycosuria did not differ significantly (p > .05) across the two groups at any of the data collection points, with six experimental and five control patients having glycosuria at some point in the study. It is of interest to note that no information concerning either the presence or absence of glycosuria was available in the medical record at any point during the two-year study for 20 of the 80 (25.0 percent) experimental patients, while this percentage was greater for the control group (22 of 51 patients, or 43.1 percent). A greater tendency to check for glycosuria seemed to exist in the experimental condition.

Organic Heart Disease

There were 166 experimental and 170 control patients who had organic heart disease at some point during the NUCRSS study. Of the 166 experimental patients, eight patients were known dead and 41 patients had been hospitalized, transferred to another clinic, had moved, or had left for unknown reasons by the end of the two-year period. For the control group, 6 patients had died while 46 had left for the other reasons mentioned.

Tables 5.1 and 5.2 contain baseline information for patients with organic heart disease. Differences between the experimental and control groups were relatively small for the incidence of hypertension, obesity, and pulmonary disease. Also, the distribution of males and females, patient age, and racial distribution differed little between groups. Despite random assignment of patients to groups, incidence of renal disease, incidence of diabetes, fee schedule distribution, CPR chart weight, and months spent at CPR clinics prior to the study displayed relatively high chance differences across conditions, as did the total number of tracer diseases present for a given patient. The effects of these differences between groups are dealt with in each of the analyses below.

Process of Care. The following four indicator variables were collected for all patients with organic heart disease—whether or not patient blood pressure, patient weight, presence of edema, and heart rhythms were checked at each visit during the period. Data for each of these variables, when condensed into tables for Year 1 only, Year 2 only, both years, and neither year showed virtually no difference in distribution between the experimental and control groups. This lack of interpretable distinction between groups was characteristic of the results when these variables were analyzed at different levels of the baseline variables mentioned above.

Another process-of-care index, a test for serum lipids or cholesterol (lipids or triglycerides for Year 1), was recorded for patients with an etiology of arteriosclerosis. The distribution for when the tests were done (i.e., in the first year only, the second year only, both years, and not done) was found to differ significantly across the experimental (N = 92) and control (N = 93) groups ($X^2[3]$ = 8.9, p = .03), favoring the experimental group (see Table 5.3). The most noticeable difference was in the "not done" category, with 21 experimental patients not receiving the test and 40 control patients not receiving the test (22.8 percent versus 43.0 percent). When this index was analyzed at varying levels of the baseline variables noted above, the experimental group always received more tests percentagewise, despite differences in baseline values. Statistical significance for the difference between groups was lost in a number of these specific analyses, at least in part due to reduced sample sizes.

For patients with an etiology of hypertension, the incidences of three different laboratory examinations are presented in Table 5.3. The distribution across the four categories differed significantly between the groups for the blood urea nitrogen or creatinine test ($X^2[3]$ = 14.5, p = .00) and for the funduscopic examination ($X^2[3]$ = 6.9, p = .03), but not for the examination of potassium ($X^2[3[$ = 1.9, p > .05). All three indices suggest better care for the experimental group.

When considering the possible effects of baseline differences between groups, the most likely differences to influence these results would be the higher incidence of both renal disease and diabetes in the experimental group, possibly resulting in a higher percentage of tests. For patients with diabetes (N = 48), the above tests that were statistically significant remained significant (p < .05) for the analyses based on the smaller samples. For patients without diabetes (N = 112), differences in distributions for the above tests indicated better care for the experimental group, though the difference was statistically significant only for the blood urea nitrogen or creatinine test. Although experimental patients both with (N = 33) and without (N = 137) renal disease received more tests, the distributions remained statistically significant only for patients without renal disease. The small number of patients with renal disease (22 experimental, 11 control) no doubt contributed to the loss of statistical significance.

TABLE 5.3   Incidence of Laboratory Examinations for Patients with Heart Disease

Etiology/Examination/Condition	Test Status			
	Done Year 1 Only	Done Year 2 Only	Done Both Years	Not Done
Hypertension				
Blood urea nitrogen or creatinine				
experimental	25 (27.5)[a]	29 (31.9)	27 (29.7)	10 (11.0)
control	9 (11.4)	25 (31.6)	20 (25.3)	25 (31.6)
Funduscopic				
experimental	—	65 (71.4)	1 (1.1)	25 (27.5)
control	—	41 (51.9)	1 (1.3)	37 (46.8)
Potassium				
experimental	17 (18.7)	24 (26.4)	22 (24.2)	28 (30.8)
control	14 (17.7)	17 (21.5)	16 (20.3)	32 (40.5)
Arteriosclerosis				
Serum lipids or triglycerides[b]				
experimental	19 (20.7)	31 (33.7)	21 (22.8)	21 (22.8)
control	13 (14.0)	26 (28.0)	14 (15.1)	40 (43.0)

a. percentages in parenthesis
b. triglycerides replaced by cholesterol for second year

For the other baseline differences between groups, both the BUN or creatinine test and the funduscopic examination occurred more frequently in the experimental group at different levels of the baseline variables. As would be expected, statistical significance was lost for a number of these small sample analyses. Because the direction of the results remained unchanged after baseline differences had been considered, data broken down along baseline dimensions are not given, since this would greatly complicate the presentation.

Outcome of Care. Three variables associated with the outcome of care have been analyzed for all patients with organic heart disease (see Table 5.4). Each of these variables marks the presence or absence of a specific defect (murmur, edema, or arrhythmia) at the beginning and/or at the end of the study. In all instances there was not a statistically significant difference ($p > .05$) across conditions for the incidence of occurrence either at the beginning or at the end of the study. Incorporating the baseline dimensions noted above into the analysis made no substantive difference in results.

Another index of outcome in the data base was the change in the status of the electrocardiogram (ECG) during the first year and during the second year. These results are also presented in Table 5.4. During the first year the control group had both more worse ECGs (14 [26.4 percent] versus 11 [18.6 percent]) and more improved ECGs (12 [22.6 percent] versus 7 [11.9 percent]). During the second year, the results indicate that at a statistically significant level ($X^2 [2] = 9.3$, $p = .01$), the experimental group had both fewer worse ECGs (8 [12.7 percent] versus 20 [33.3 percent]) and more improved ECGs (13 [20.6 percent] versus 5 [8.3 percent]). Once again, when ECG change was analyzed at different values of baseline variables, the direction of the effect of the MIS was the same, though the analysis at certain values of the baseline variables resulted in a loss of significance for the second-year difference between groups.

Both systolic and diastolic blood pressure records were taken at various points during the study for heart disease patients with an etiology of hypertension. The use of the MIS did not improve the status of hypertension. Ending diastolic blood

TABLE 5.4   Presence of Heart Defects for Patients with Organic Heart Disease and Change in Electrocardiogram (ECG) for All Patients with Test Available

Time/Condition	Murmur[a]		Edema[a]		Arrhythmia[a]	
	Present	Not Present	Present	Not Present	Present	Not Present
Beginning of study						
experimental (N = 166)	65 (53.3)[b]	57 (46.7)	16 (15.4)	88 (84.6)	16 (14.3)	96 (85.7)
control (N = 170)	67 (54.9)	55 (45.1)	26 (25.5)	76 (74.5)	20 (18.3)	89 (81.7)
End of study						
experimental (N = 166)	58 (58.6)	41 (41.4)	20 (23.8)	64 (76.2)	26 (38.8)	41 (61.2)
control (N = 170)	52 (58.4)	37 (41.6)	25 (28.4)	63 (71.6)	27 (43.5)	35 (56.5)

Year/Condition	Better ECG	Same ECG	Worse ECG
Change during first year			
experimental	7 (11.9)	41 (69.5)	11 (18.6)
control	12 (22.6)	27 (50.9)	14 (26.4)
Change during second year			
experimental	13 (20.6)	42 (66.7)	8 (12.7)
control	5 (8.3)	35 (58.3)	20 (33.3)

a. Patients not appearing in either category had no information available.
b. Percentages of non-missing cases are in parenthesis.

pressure means were 144.7 (N = 60, SD = 25.3) for the experimental group and 150.3 (N = 46, SD = 26.6) for the control group. Ending diastolic means were 91.6 (N = 60, SD = 13.0) and 94.8 (N = 46, SD = 14.6) for the gwo groups, respectively.

DISCUSSION

This chapter described a study utilizing a methodological approach called the tracer methodology that was originally proposed as an alternative to implicit peer review. The method was applied in a modified form using a randomized experimental design to assess the direct impact of MIS technology on patient care. Discussion of the results of this study will embrace two interconnected themes—the actual impact that the MIS had on patient care and the suitability of the tracer methodology for detecting that impact.

Analysis of data for the two tracer diseases examined, diabetes and organic heart disease, would seem to indicate the following. The MIS has had little influence on either the process or outcome of care for diabetic patients. There was no statistically significant difference between the experimental and control patients for the occurrence of a blood sugar examination or the administration/review of diet, and these conditions were similar on mean blood sugar level and the occurrence of glycosuria. However, the data do suggest better process of care, with perhaps a small improvement in outcome for patients with organic heart disease. Experimental patients received a significantly greater number of tests for serum lipids or cholesterol (lipids or triglycerides for Year 1). Further, experimental patients with organic heart disease and hypertension received a greater number of blood urea nitrogen (or creatinine) examinations and funduscopic examinations. Although there was little difference between conditions in terms of heart-related defects, morc improved ECGs were present among the experimental patients by the second year.

It was noted earlier that several other tracer diseases were employed in the larger evaluation of the present MIS, and though not yet available in detail, results for these tracer diseases seem to confirm our present conclusion. For example, the MIS had little influence on blood pressure but did positively influence weight loss for obese patients and the urine test outcomes for patients with renal disease. Evidence for better process of care was found in all three of the aforementioned tracer areas—hypertension, renal disease, and obesity.

That the MIS had an impact on the process of care and, to a lesser extent, the outcome of care, is reasonably clear. Although further research will be needed to define specifically the mechanisms responsible for MIS-related changes, a hypothesis can be offered now. With reference to heart disease, improvement apparently has resulted because the MIS brings to the attention of physicians the need for various medical procedures that should routinely be performed. The procedures we recorded are a part of a set of standards based on the literature and agreement among Northwestern specialists (Haring et al., 1974). The MIS reminds physicians that recommended procedures are either needed or out-of-date, and apparently they respond by ordering these procedures.

Results of a study by McDonald (1976a) seem to support this hypothesis. In that study, one group of physicians was presented for several days (1) computer-generated recommendations and reminders for the care of patients, (2) a computer-tailored encounter form containing active prescriptions, and (3) a summary report of the medical record for each patient that was seen. During the latter half of the study the physicians were presented with only items 2 and 3. A second group of physicians was given MIS output in the reverse order—during the first part of the study, items 2 and 3 (partial information), and during the latter part, 1, 2, and 3 (complete information). The presence of the computer-generated recommendations and reminders reduced the number of errors in medical reasoning regardless of the physician's experience or the order of partial and complete information (i.e., there was no "training" effect resulting from prior exposure to the MIS recommendations). McDonald concludes that the MIS reduces information overload, and this reduction, rather than making medical reasoning deficient, is responsible for the decreased error rate. In light of

McDonald's conclusion, it is worth restating that the present findings occurred using a MIS that generated recommendations and reminders as well as a summary of the medical record.

Methodological Issues

Before considering other matters, a final comment is offered concerning baseline differences that emerged by chance between the experimental and control patients. A preferred randomization scheme would have been to stratify patients by disease area (diabetes, heart disease, and so on) as well as important psychosocial variables (e.g., age, race), and then to assign patients randomly to conditions out of each strata (a procedure often called "blocking"). That was not done, since the larger study was designed before the tracer methodology was developed. However, we should note difficulties that accompany such a procedure. For example, patients often fall into multiple disease areas and/or acquire an additional disease classification during the course of the study. In retrospect, partial blocking might have been performed even by disease areas, had multiple classifications been used (heart disease, obesity, and renal disease; heart disease, obesity, and diabetes; and so on). Instead, we used simple randomization and then retrospectively compared the experimental and control groups on relevant baseline parameters.

Even though chance variation produced some baseline differences that were large enough to be of concern to us, the subsequent subdivision of patients along a given baseline dimension made no substantive difference in the results of the analysis. For example, when patients with organic heart disease were subdivided into groups with and without diabetes, the same conclusion was reached as when diabetic and nondiabetic patients were analyzed together. Regardless of whether or not baseline parameters were included in the analysis, experimental patients evidenced at a statistically significant level a greater number of blood urea nitrogen and creatinine tests, funduscopic examinations, and examinations of potassium. Although statistical significance was lost in some small sample analyses that incorporated baseline parameters, the direction of the effect was always the same as when baseline differences were ignored. We have concluded that the MIS, not baseline discrepancies occurring by chance, was responsible for the differences in the process and outcome of care that we have reported.

The use of the tracer methodology has allowed us to assess the direct impact of MIS technology on patient care. MIS technology is broadly based relative to more specialized technologies, such as the computerized acquisition of physiological signals or interpretation of laboratory tests. Nonetheless, MIS and other broadly based technologies (e.g., computerized knowledge bases and medical decision systems, occupational health monitoring systems) should not escape evaluation at the level of direct impact on the patient. The tracer methodology, by focusing on important disease entities, offers an objective way to accomplish this end.

Number of Tracers. Our data indicate that results vary considerably over tracer areas. For example, if general conclusion concerning the impact of MIS were drawn from an examination of diabetes alone, a very different conclusion, one of no effect whatsoever, would be drawn. Most technologies, and particularly those having a broad basis for potential impact, cannot be viewed as entirely positive or negative in effect. To make claims for or against new technologies on the basis of findings in one or two tracer areas would seem imprudent. This, of course, leads to the question, "Which and how many tracer areas are needed?" The answer will obviously depend on the medical environment and specific technology under review, but one comment does seem in order. The data thus far indicate that the tracer methodology is more sensitive to changes in process of care than outcome of care, no doubt due to what is often an unclear causal relationship between these.

Studies attempting to relate process and outcome of care (Brooks, 1973; Lyons and Payne, 1974; Romm et al., 1976; Starfield and Scheff, 1972; Kane et al., 1977) have so far met with only mixed success. Our position is that a technological innovation that improves the application of current medical thinking should not be ruled out because current practices are not as effective as they might be. The hope is that medical procedures will continually improve, and the worth of technologies like MIS should be judged primarily on the basis of how well they aid the implementation of what currently is considered to be good medicine. This, then, suggests that a good tracer area will be one where the currently recommended process of care is intricate enough to afford opportunities for violations. Otherwise a sensitive and meaningful (perhaps the best) indicator of technological impact—i.e., process-of-care measurements—will be subject to what often is termed a ceiling effect. That is, improvement cannot occur where there is no room for improvement, and this will eliminate some disease areas for use as tracers as well as some parameters of outcome of care.

Our concluding comment concerns the potential role that the tracer methodology could play in the cost-benefit analysis of new technologies generally and MIS specifically. It is clearly the case that a calculation of the monetary impact of a new medical technology must include parameters reflecting resultant changes in the medical procedures extended to patients. Operating costs alone are not sufficient. For example, Rogers and Haring (1979) have shown that automating the medical record reduced the average hospital stay of patients with computerized records, while, in agreement with the present data, the overall number of laboratory examinations increased. Here, two cost-related variables, one reflecting the outcome of care and the other the process of care, are moving in opposite directions. The net effect could not be determined in this instance because cost data were not collected along with process-of-care and outcome-of-care data. It is enough for the present point, however, to note that the impact of MIS on patient care per se must be considered along with operating and administrative financial data if a comprehensive cost-benefit analysis is to be achieved. The tracer methodology, by producing objective data over the course of a disease episode, provides a method for including in the cost-benefit equation any changes in medical care, and, it is hoped, corresponding changes in outcome of care, that a technological innovation might produce.

REFERENCES

Battele Columbus Laboratories (1976) "Evaluation of a medical information system in a community hospital." DHEW Publication (HRA) 76-3144. Washington, DC: Government Printing Office.

BEILIN, L. J., C. J. BULPITT, E. C. COLES, C. T. DOLLERY, B. F. JOHNSON, C. MEARNS, and A. D. MUNRO-RAURE, and S. C. TURNER (1974) "Computer-based hypertension clinical records: a co-operative study." British Medical Journal 2: 212-216.

BRADSHAW-SMITH, J. H. (1976) "A computer record-keeping system for general practice." British Medical Journal 1: 1395-1397.

BROOKS, R. H. (1973) "Quality of care assessment: a comparison of five methods of peer review." DHEW Publication (HRA) 74-3100. Washington, DC: Government Printing Office.

BULPITT, C. J., L. J. BEILIN, E. C. COLES, C. T. DOLLERY, B. F. JOHNSON, A. D. MUNRO-FAURE, and S. C. TURNER (1976) "Randomized controlled trial of computer-held medical records in hypertensive patients." British Medical Journal 1: 677-699.

COBELLI, C. and A. SALVAN (1975) "A medical record and a computer program for diagnosis of thyroid disease." Methods of Information in Medicine 14: 126-132.

EHRENHAFT, P. M., S. CORCORAN, E. A. HARWOOD, and H. WEST (1977) Policy Implications of Medical Information Systems. Washington, DC: Office of Technology Assessment.

GREENBURG, A. G., M. GOLDBERT, D. J. WERNER, K. E. JANDA, and O. M. HARING (1971) "Medical summaries from computerized data bases," pp. 189-196 in Proceedings of the San Diego Bio-Medical Symposium 10.

GROSSMAN, J. H., G. O. BARNETT, T. D. KOEPSELL, H. R. NESSON, J. L. DORSEY, and R. R. PHILLIPS (1973) "An automated medical record system." Journal of the American Medical Association 224: 1616-1621.

HARING, O. M. (1973) "A problem oriented record symmary for use in the clinic." Chicago Medicine 76: 1002.

———, G. W. MIDDLEKAUF, and L. SECHREST (1974) "An internal auditing system for improving the quality of medical care." Journal of the American Medical Women's Association 28: 178-187.

KANE, R. L., J. GARDNER, D. D. WRIGHT, G. SNELL, D. SUNDWALL, and F. R. WOOLLEY (1977) "Relationship between process and outcome in ambulatory care." Medical Care 15: 961-965.

KENNEDY, F., J. J. CLEARY, A. D. ROY, and A. W. KAY (1968) " 'Switch': a system producing a full hospital case history on computer." Lancet 2: 1230-1233.

KESSNER, D. M., C. E. KALK, and J. SINGER (1973) "Assessing health quality— the case for tracers." New England Journal of Medicine 288, 4: 189-194.

LEBOW, J. L. (1974) "Consumer assessments of the quality of medical care." Medical Care 12: 328-337.

LYONS, T. F. and B. C. PAYNE (1974) "The relationship of physicians' medical recording performance to their medical care performance." Medical Care 12: 463-469.

McAULIFFE, W. E. (1979) "Measuring the quality of medical care: process vs. outcome." Milbank Memorial Fund Quarterly/Health and Society 57: 118-152.

——— (1978) "Studies of process-outcome correlations in medical care evaluations: a critique." Medical Care 16: 907-930.

McDONALD, C. J. (1976a) "Protocol-based computer reminders, the quality of care and the non-perfectability of man." New England Journal of Medicine 295: 1351-1355.

——— (1976b) "Use of a computer to detect and respond to clinical events: Its effect on clinical behavior." Annals of Internal Medicine 84: 162-167.

———, R. MURRAY, D. JERIS, B. BHARGAVA, J. SEEGER, and L. BLEVINS (1977) "A computer-based record and clinical monitoring system for ambulatory care." American Journal of Public Health 67: 240-245.

MELLNER, C., H. SELANDER, and J. WOLODARSKI (1976) "The computerized problem-oriented medical record at Karolinska Hospital—format and function, user's acceptance and patient attitude to questionnaire." Methods of Information in Medicine 15: 11-200.

National Center for Health Services Research [NCHSR] Research Digest Series (1977) "Automation of the problem-oriented medical record." DHEW Publication (HRA) 77-3177. Washington, DC: Government Printing Office.

NOVICK, L., K. DICKINSON, R. ASNES, S. P. MAY LAN, and R. LOWENSTEIN (1976) "Assessment of ambulatory care: application of the tracer methodology." Medical Care 14: 1-12.

ROGERS, J. L. and O. M. HARING (1979) "The impact of a computerized medical record summary system in incidence and length of hospitalization." Medical Care 17, 6: 618-630.

ROMM, R. J., B. S. HULKA, and F. MAYO (1976) "Correlates of outcome in patients with congestive heart failure." Medical Care 14: 765-776.

SCHENTHAL, J. E., J. W. SWEENEY, and W. J. NETTLETON (1960) "Clinical applications of large scale electronic data processing apparatus I." Journal of the American Medical Association 173: 6-11.

SCHENTHAL, J. E., J. W. SWEENEY, W. J. NETTLETON, and R. D. YODER (1963) "Clinical applications of large scale electronic data processing apparatus III." Journal of the American Medical Association 186: 101-105.

SCHMIDT, E. C., D. W. SCHALL, and C. C. MORRISON (1974) "Computerized problem-oriented medical record for ambulatory practice." Medical Care 12: 316-327.

SLACK, W. V., G. P. HICKS, C. E. REED, and L. J. VAN CURA (1966) "A computer based medical history system." New England Journal of Medicine 274: 194-198.

STARFIELD, B. and D. SCHEFF (1972) "Effectiveness of pediatric care: the relationship between process and outcome." Pediatrics 49: 547-552.

STARFIELD, B., D. SIMBORG, C. JOHNS, and S. HORN (1977) "Coordination of care and its relationship to continuity and medical records." Medical Care 15: 929-938.

WIEKHAM, J.E.A., C.A.C. CHARLTON, B. RICHARDS, W. F. HENDRY, J. P. WARD, E.P.N. O'DONOGHUE, R. G. HAMSHERE, and D. A. FRANKLIN (1975) "A computer-based record and organization system for a department of urology." British Journal of Urology 47: 345-357.

WILLIAMSON, J. (1971) "Evaluating quality of patient care." Journal of the American Medical Association 218: 564-569.

ZIELSTORFF, R. D., J. L. ROGLIERI, K. D. MARBLE, J. W. POINTRAS, F. VAN DEUSEN, S. M. FOLLAYTTAR, and G. O. BARNETT (1977) "Experience with a computer-based medical record for nurse practitioners in ambulatory care." Computer Biomedical Research 10: 61-74.

Mark S. Thompson
Alan B. Cohen

Harvard School of Public Health

6

DECISION ANALYSIS
Electronic Fetal Monitoring

INTRODUCTION

Evaluations of new medical technologies are intended to reduce uncertainty about their efficacy, their risks, and their costs. Determining the optimal evaluation strategy depends on a sensitive understanding of the uncertainty about these parameters. Yet such uncertainty remains exceptionally difficult to describe, to model, and to reflect appropriately in decision-making.

This chapter addresses the uncertainty associated with one recent medical innovation: electronic fetal monitoring (EFM). Among the many variants of EFM, we concentrate on the most common: direct internal monitoring of the fetal heart rate via a

AUTHORS' NOTE: This chapter is based on a presentation made on October 18, 1979, at the Third Annual Meeting of the Evaluation Research Society in Minneapolis. The constructive comments made by Peter Braun, M.D., Eric Fortess, M.P.H., S.M., Howard Frazier, M.D., Joan Meier, Raymond Neutra, M.D., Dr.P.H., and Bruce Young, M.D., and the research assistance of Joan Meier are gratefully acknowledged. The work was supported by grants from the Robert Wood Johnson Foundation and the Commonwealth Fund to the Center for the Analysis of Health Practices, and by Grant SOC-77-16602 of the National Science Foundation.

spiral electrode attached to the fetal scalp, and monitoring of labor contraction pressure via an intrauterine catheter or an external tocodynamometer. Such monitoring is designed to detect fetal hypoxia and to enable timely corrective actions to be taken. These actions include repositioning of the mother (and, indirectly, the fetus), administration of oxygen and intravenous fluids, and—in otherwise irremediable cases—delivery by cesarean section.

History and Current Status of EFM

Fetal scalp electrocardiography was developed by Hon (1960) and became broadly commercially available in the late 1960s. Use of monitoring expanded throughout the 1970s and, by 1975, most obstetric residency training programs in Canada and the United States had monitoring equipment. One survey of all 360 residency training programs found that 278 of 279 respondents employed EFM methods (Dilts, 1976). At the present time, it is estimated that 60 to 70 percent of all births in this country are monitored electronically (Obstetrical Practices in the United States, 1978). Compared with many other medical innovations, EFM has been extensively evaluated. Four randomized, controlled trials (RCTs) have been carried out (Haverkamp et al., 1976; Renou et al., 1976; Kelso et al., 1978; Haverkamp et al., 1979), and hundreds of articles on monitoring have appeared in the professional literature.

The rapid dissemination of this technology seems to indicate confidence that it is, on balance, beneficial. Closer examination, however, reveals considerably divergent assessments. Individual obstetricians and articles are often certain in their assessments; it is only in encountering other obstetricians and other articles— comparably certain but in discrepant positions—that a sense of the overall uncertainty is obtained. In the following sections we will investigate the range and the implications of this uncertainty.

METHODS

The methodology used here represents extensions of several current techniques. To identify and to quantify uncertainty, we follow a course allied to the current use of consensus development conferences (National Institutes of Health, 1978) and survey broadly both the literature and informed professional opinion. As in these conferences, we seek to derive best estimates of various parameters—recognizing that these derivations must, to some extent, involve discretionary judgments. Unlike the conferences, however, we stress the importance of gauging the ranges of uncertainty associated with the estimates.

The type of uncertainty that concerns us may be illustrated by the question of the effects of EFM on perinatal mortality. We are interested in knowing both the best estimate of the effects and the range of judgments about this best estimate. Some responsible obstetricians believe the effect is as low as zero, while others believe it as high as a saving of 9.4 lives per 1000 births. Both groups can cite substantial references from the literature in support of their positions. We consider the range of uncertainty to extend from 0 to 9.4 lives saved per 1000 births. We determine these ranges by processes similar to those used in obtaining best estimates: considered, but inevitably discretionary, judgments based on the best available data. Put another way, the consensus development conferences focus on best point estimates of parameters; we focus on the variability or confidence interval for those estimates and its implications.

To investigate the consequences of uncertainty, we similarly extend the current techniques of clinical decision analysis and of benefit-cost analysis. Those methods traditionally are used to identify best courses of action—in the present case, whether or not to monitor. We make such determinations but are not so much interested in them as in the extent to which they vary depending on the components of uncertainty. This variability is measured by comparing the results of clinical decision analysis and of benefit-cost analysis obtained under alternative assumptions.

Obtaining Estimates of Uncertainty

Parer (1978) identified as possible benefits of electronic fetal monitoring: decreased perinatal mortality, improved neonatal neurologic outcome (reduced brain damage), and influence on litigation. He cited as potential risks: increased maternal morbidity, increased neonatal morbidity, increased cesarean sectioning, and dehumanization of the birth process. To estimate the uncertainty associated with each of these factors, we relied on reviews of the professional literature and on interviews with practicing obstetricians. The literature contained few articles on issues of litigation and dehumanization, and the obstetricians whom we interviewed were uncomfortable in quantifying the importance of these concerns. We concentrated accordingly on estimating possible effects on five parameters: perinatal mortality, brain damage, maternal infections, neonatal infections, and cesarean sectioning. Maternal mortality resulting from sectioning is, due to lack of data, treated in a slightly different manner. This emphasis is in line with the approach adopted in other current reviews of the technology (Banta and Thacker, 1979a; National Institutes of Health, 1979).

Literature Review. Seven studies, among the hundreds in the literature of monitoring, seem especially important. These include the only four RCTs, noted above, one retrospective epidemiological analysis with explicit control for risk (Neutra et al., 1978), and the two comprehensive and interpretive reviews of the literature noted above (Banta and Thacker, 1979a; National Institutes of Health, 1979). These were accorded somewhat greater weight in our review. There is, however, no question that other, less rigorously designed studies have strongly influenced current obstetrical perceptions (see chapter by Wortman). These too were included in estimating the ranges of uncertainty.

Upper and lower bounds to the ranges of uncertainty were derived by asking what were the maximum and minimum parameter estimates for which one could make cogent cases. We felt that, for the most part, estimates based on single, possibly idiosyncratic studies were not convincing. We accordingly sought estimates that could be defended on the basis of a number of studies. Best estimates within the range of uncertainty were arrived at by reviewing the evidence, by weighting more heavily those studies which were based on larger samples or which had fewer threats to their experimental validity, and, occasionally, by reanalyzing the data. The best estimates are inevitably subjective, since both the upper and lower bounds were chosen by the criterion that reasonable cases could be made for them.

Obstetrician Interviews. Twenty-three practicing obstetricians and one practicing neonatologist (all henceforth referred to as "obstetricians") in the greater Boston area were involved. This sample included six chiefs of obstetric services. The interviews were based on a prepared questionnaire, yet did not run as smoothly as had been hoped. We intended to obtain estimates of the uncertainty in the responses of individual obstetricians. An ideal would have been to describe uncertainty in terms of probability distribution functions. Unfortunately, while the obstetricians were generally willing to give numerical estimates of probabilities and, less frequently, of values, they were reluctant to estimate the uncertainty associated with their responses. We were, as a result, forced to gauge uncertainty as the differences among obstetricians rather than as the uncertainty associated by them with their own estimates.

Selection of the interview sample was guided by availability of the doctors and by a desire for representativeness. We consciously included proponents and opponents of EFM in the sample. This strategy would not yield accurate estimates of the proportions of obstetricians taking various positions on EFM, but would indicate the range of disagreement among them. This was our primary goal. We report the high, low, and median obstetrician estimates for each of the five parameters studied.

With estimates on the ranges of uncertainty, we sought to analyze how this uncertainty would affect decision-making through the alternative approaches of clinical decision analysis and benefit-cost analysis.

Clinical Decision Analysis

An appropriate mode of decision-making for obstetricians and parents is that of clinical decision analysis (Weinstein and Fineberg, forthcoming). In this framework, the decision maker compares alternative obstetric outcomes—how good and bad they are relative to each other—and chooses actions that offer best outcomes on expectation.

Clinical decision analysis requires subjective judgments on the values of alternative outcomes: perinatal death, brain damage, maternal death, various morbidities, and cesarean delivery. We elicited these values by interviewing 21 persons, including 7 male obstetricians, 4 other male physicians, 3 lay males, and 7 lay females. Of the interviewees, 5, including 2 of the obstetricians, were Roman Catholics. As with the obstetrician interviews, this was not a representative sample, nor was it intended to be. An attempt was made to obtain a broad spectrum of opinion. Two typical questions used to elicit values were:

Suppose that an action that would avert severe mental retardation for sure carried risk of maternal death. What is the maximum risk acceptable?

Suppose that an action would lead to a certain fetal scalp infection in order to eliminate a small chance of severe mental retardation. By how much must the chance of severe mental retardation be reduced to justify the action?

With the values obtained in this way, we were able to calculate—using clinical decision analysis—whether monitoring was or was not desirable for the average monitored birth. This is the usual type of objective of clinical decision analysis. Our main goal, however, was to gauge the potential impact of uncertainty on the monitoring decision. To this end, we examined the differences between the expected values obtained if each parameter were truly at the upper-bound value from the literature and if it were at the lower-bound value. This enabled comparison of the importance of the uncertainty associated with the five parameters studied.

Benefit-Cost Analysis

Monetary concerns have, at best, tangential impact on clinical decision analysis. However, for a society deciding whether the investment required for fetal monitoring is justified—especially in the light of alternative uses for the money—financial concerns are central. We used benefit-cost analysis to evaluate the comparative importance of financial and nonfinancial factors in deciding whether to monitor.[1]

In benefit-cost analysis, the value of limited medical problems is taken as the expense of dealing with them. The values of mortality are the present-valued (discounted) earnings forgone, while the value of mental retardation is forgone earnings plus treatment costs. These dollar values are shown in Table 6.1. All values but that of averting mental retardation derive from Banta and Thacker (1979a). That value is obtained by using the results of Conley and Milunsky (1975) to modify the value of Banta and Thacker. Critical commentary on the numbers used by Banta and Thacker is to be found in Hobbins et al. (1979). All discounting, following Banta and Thacker, is at 10 percent.[2]

Measurement of the potential effect of uncertainty in benefit-cost analysis proceeded in a manner analogous to that for clinical decision analysis. The absolute importance of the uncertainty concerning each parameter was taken to be the difference between the estimated net benefits (or costs) using the upper-bound value and that using the lower-bound value.

RESULTS

Estimates of Uncertainty

The first step in calculating the clinical decision and benefit-cost analyses involves estimates of uncertainty. The estimates for the five parameters selected are presented in this section.

Perinatal Mortality. Over the decade 1966-1976, perinatal mortality declined from 32.4 to 21.2 deaths per 1000 total births (Obstetrical Practices in the United States, 1978). The extent to which the introduction of EFM during this period was responsible for the improvement is, however, unknown. The RCTs were too small to show any difference in perinatal mortality; the non-RCTs suggest, but due to confounding factors do not prove, that EFM reduced mortality. Best estimates in the literature are that EFM reduces perinatal mortality by 2.8 (Banta and Thacker, 1979a) or 3.1 (National Institutes of

TABLE 6.1   Economic Values of Various Perinatal Events Estimated as Direct Costs of Treatment or as Values of Present Discounted Future Productivity

Event	*Value*
Saving one perinatal life	$ 33,370
Averting one case of severe mental retardation	$ 57,997
Maternal death	-$114,057
Maternal infection with vaginal delivery	-$ 570
Maternal infection with cesarean delivery	-$ 1,140
Fetal scalp infection	-$ 700
Cesarean section	-$ 2,300
Direct service cost of EFM	-$ 50

SOURCES: Banta and Thacker (1979a) and Conley and Milunsky (1975).

Health, 1979) deaths per 1000 births. These figures reflect extensive analysis of the literature and are hedged with myriad qualifications. It is extremely difficult to infer from all of the many studies the way in which such figures depend on identifiable risk factors. We shall return to this point. All figures presented pertain to the monitoring of an average sample of 1000 births in the average U.S. hospital. We take the mean of the two figures, 2.95, to be our best estimate of perinatal mortality reduction via EFM.

Neither set of authors gives a confidence interval for its estimate, yet such an interval might be constructed from the figures cited in the studies reviewed. Seven studies (Kelly and Kulkarni, 1973; Edington et al., 1975; Shenker et al., 1975; Tutera and Newman, 1975; Lee and Baggish, 1976; Amato, 1977; Weinraub et al., 1978) indicate that an estimated decrease in neonatal death rates of at least 7.0 per 1000 monitored births is achieved with EFM. Four (Tutera and Newman, 1975; Lee and Baggish, 1976; Amato, 1977; Hamilton et al., 1978) found differences in intrapartum fetal mortality of 2.4 or greater in favor of EFM. Summing these to obtain the change in perinatal mortality indicates an improvement of 9.4 deaths per 1000 births via EFM. This is a reasonable upper limit of benefit based on the literature, while zero, based on the RCTs, is a reasonable lower limit.[3]

The obstetricians interviewed gave estimates ranging between 1.0 and 6.0 lives saved via EFM per 1000 births. The median estimate was 2.5. Given the state of the literature, these estimates seem reasonable. Most of the obstetricians cited published studies or figures from their own hospitals in support of their estimates.

Brain Damage. Net brain damage prevented by EFM comprises: (1) babies saved by EFM to be healthy instead of brain-damaged, less (2) babies saved by EFM to be brain-damaged instead of dead. Data on net brain damage prevented are unclear. Intrapartum difficulties are associated with severe brain damage and cerebral palsy, but the direction of causation is unclear. Most neonates suffering from intrapartum hypoxia develop normally. The Task Force on Predictors of Fetal Distress (National Institutes of Health, 1979) estimates that 1.0 case of severe brain damage (I.Q. below 50) is prevented per 1000 monitored births. A lower confidence limit of zero could be based on the various studies (Low et al., 1978; Birch et al., 1970) showing normal subsequent development in hypoxic neonates; an upper confidence limit is the figure of 2.5 cases per 1000 births of severe brain damage prevented—as estimated and used in a benefit-cost analysis by Quilligan and Paul (1975).

The obstetricians hesitated to quantify the likely gains in reducing brain damage. Most admitted that they did not know the incidence of mental retardation but estimated the proportion of it—both mild and severe retardation—that they felt EFM could prevent. Interpreting these answers accordingly, the obstetrician estimates range from 0.6 to 3.0 cases of severe brain damage prevented per 1000 monitored births, with a median of 1.7. This is somewhat but not unreasonably higher than the numbers indicated by the literature. Obstetrician estimates of mild mental retardation prevented by EFM range from 6 to 25 cases prevented per 1000 monitorings, with a median of 15. These latter estimates are far in excess of any experimental findings and seem to overlook the role of environmental factors in mild retardation.

Maternal Infections. EFM may cause maternal infections, primarily endometritis. We obtain best estimates of infection rates by combining the results of seven studies (Haverkamp et al., 1976; Chan et al., 1973; Wiechetek et al., 1974; Hagen, 1975; Gassner and Ledger, 1976; Gibbs et al., 1976, 1978). Without EFM, best estimates are that endometritis occurs in 1.6 percent of women delivering vaginally and in 28.5 percent of women undergoing cesarean section. With EFM and vaginal delivery, infection rates vary between 1.3 and 3.6 percent, with one outlier at 11.2 percent. We take 1.3 and 5.0 as reasonable bounds to the best estimate. The best estimate is the mean rate found in combining the results of three studies (Haverkamp et al., 1976, 1979; Gassner and Ledger, 1976). This rate is 3.7 percent.

Rates of infection among EFM patients undergoing cesarean delivery were found in two RCTs (Haverkamp et al., 1976, 1979) to be 23.7 and 1.5 percent—the difference apparently due to antibiotic prophylaxis in the latter study. Four non-RCTs (Hagen, 1975; Gassner and Ledger, 1976; Gibbs et al., 1976, 1978) found rates of 40.4, 44.0, 48.3, and 54.5 percent. The mean rate found in six studies (Haverkamp et al., 1976, 1979; Hagen, 1975; Gassner and Ledger, 1976; Gibbs et al., 1976, 1978) was 42.2 percent. We take this as our best estimate with reasonable bounds of 24 and 48 percent.

Obstetrician estimates of the infections caused by EFM for vaginally delivered mothers ranged from zero to 3 percent, with a median of 0.5 percent. These estimates are somewhat more favorable to EFM than the data in the literature, but are not unreasonable; they are derived, for the most part, from personal experience. Causation in this area is especially difficult to judge, inasmuch as (1) the EFM and non-EFM groups are not comparable, and (2) different hospital practices such as the use of prophylactic antibiotics significantly affect infection rates.

Neonatal Infections. The spiral scalp electrode used in EFM may cause scalp abscesses. These rarely become complicated and often are not noticed or recorded. Three studies (Paul and Hon, 1973; Feder et al., 1976; Plavidal and Werch, 1976) found rates of scalp abscess ranging between 0.4 and 0.9 percent. A fourth study (Okada et al., 1977) looked more closely for the infections—clipping the hair about the electrode site and inspecting the site daily. It identified infections in 4.5 percent of all births. The rate of normally noticeable infections would be estimated from the literature at 0.5 percent, with bounds of 0.4 and 0.9 percent. Obstetrician estimates ranged from 0.1 to 5.0 percent, with a median of 0.15 percent.

Cesarean Sectioning. Nationally, the cesarean section rate (CSR) increased from 5.0 to 11.4 percent between 1968 and 1976 (Obstetrical Practices in the United States, 1978). This period also saw a vast growth in the use of EFM, which has often been linked with the increase in the CSR. Confounding the picture has been a concomitant rise in the CSR for cephalopelvic disproportion, breech presentations, and other difficult obstetric situations—all theoretically unrelated to EFM. The three RCTs for high-risk cases (Haverkamp et al., 1976, 1979; Renou et al., 1976) found that cesarean sectioning increased with EFM by 5.8 to 12.0 cases per 100 births. The lone RCT (Kelso et al., 1978) for low-risk births found 5.1 more cesareans per 100 births with EFM. The observed greater rate of cesareans in non-RCTs (with noncomparable populations in the EFM and non-EFM groups) ranged from 2.5 to 9.7 more cesareans per 100 births. Weighting the RCT results by sample size and by the proportions of high- and low-risk births (20 and 80 percent) yields an estimated 5.8 additional cesareans for EFM per 100 births without previous cesarean. This is consistent with the non-RCT results. Banta and Thacker (1979a) obtained an estimate of 6.0 by assuming that one-half of the difference in cesareans between 1965 and 1975 was due to EFM. The Task Force on Predictors of Fetal Distress (National Institutes of Health, 1979) did not develop consensus on this point, but instead made the following points: (1) There were significant differences between the EFM and non-EFM groups in two of the RCTs; (2) an increased CSR due to EFM could be due primarily to fetal distress, and cesareans for fetal distress have increased minimally; and (3) an analysis of one set of unpublished retrospective data indicated that EFM increased the CSR by only 3.0 per 1000 births. We take 32 per 1000 births without previous cesarean to be a reasonable estimate of the CSR increase due to EFM (splitting the difference between the figures of 60 and 3 cited above). Reasonable lower and upper bounds are 3 and 99 (two RCTs found a difference at least this great).

The obstetricians were unwilling to quantify the change in CSR due to EFM. Many cited situations in which EFM might have the effect of averting cesareans that would be performed without EFM. Those feeling that EFM increased the CSR counterbalanced those feeling that EFM decreased it, leading to a median estimate of zero effect. To gauge the maternal mortality resulting from cesarean section, we adopted the estimate of one study (Evrard and Gold, 1977) that the average cesarean section has .00031 chance of causing maternal death. Insufficient data were available to gauge the uncertainty associated with maternal mortality, as estimated for other variables of interest. Table 6.2 presents a summary of the best parameter estimates based on the literature and on the obstetrician interviews.

Clinical Decision Analysis

Table 6.3 shows the median values of alternative obstetric outcomes estimated by our interviewees. The median answer to the first sample question quoted above was that a risk of maternal death of up to one in 300 was acceptable to prevent a sure case of severe mental retardation. This led to the entry in

TABLE 6.2   Comparison of Estimates on EFM Parameters Derived from the Literature and from Interviews with Obstetricians[a]

Parameter	Estimates in Literature: Lower Bound, Best Estimate, Upper Bound	Obstetrician Estimates: Lower Bound, Median, Upper Bound
1. Reduction in perinatal morality	0.0, 2.95, 9.4	1.0, 2.5, 6.0
2. Reduction in severe mental retardation	0.0, 1.0, 2.5	0.6, 1.7, 3.0
3. Increase in infections for vaginally delivered mothers	-3, 21, 34	0, 5, 30
4. Increase in neonatal infections	4, 5, 9	1, 1.5, 50
5. Increase in cesarean section rate (CSR)	3, 32, 99	U, O, U[b]

a. All figures are cases per 1000 monitorings in an average sample of births in an average U.S. hospital by EFM. The denominator is births for 1, 2, 4, and 5, and mothers for 3.
b. U = unquantified

Table 6.3 indicating that maternal death is considered 300 times worse than incurring a case of severe mental retardation. (Respondents pointed out that the answer depends on maternal age, the presence of other children, and other factors. The figure of 300 was estimated for the average situation.) Similarly, the value of $-.0001$ for a fetal scalp infection indicates that the median interviewee would accept a 100 percent certain fetal scalp infection in order to have one chance in 10,000 of averting severe mental retardation.

Quantifying Benefits and Risks. Using these values together with our best estimates of event likelihoods, we can calculate whether the average delivery should be monitored. The expected gain of perinatal mortality reduction due to EFM (EG_{PMR}) is calculated in clinical decision analysis as the likely frequency of gain multiplied by its value: $EG_{MRP} = (.00295)(.7) = .0021$. Similarly, the likely gain in preventing severe mental retardation (EG_{MRP}) is calculated to be .001 (= .001 times 1.0).

TABLE 6.3   Values of Possible Obstetrical Outcomes as Estimated by Obstetricians, Other Physicians, and Laypersons

Phenomenon Valued	*Value as Proportion of the Value in Making a Severely Retarded Baby Perfectly Healthy*
1. Saving a perinatal life	0.7
2. Making a severely retarded baby perfectly healthy	1.0
3. Nonfatal endometritis with a cesarean delivery	-.0001
4. Nonfatal endometritis with a cesarean delivery	-. 001
5. Maternal death	- 300
6. Fetal scalp infection	-.0001
7. Having an uncomplicated cesarean delivery instead of an uncomplicated vaginal delivery	-.0002

With variations in both the CSR and maternal infection rate, we calculate the maternal expectations under four scenarios. We define ME_{CM}, ME_{CU}, ME_{VM}, and ME_{VU} to be the maternal expectations, respectively, with a cesarean after monitoring, with a cesarean unmonitored, with vaginal delivery after monitoring, and with vaginal delivery unmonitored. The likelihood of maternal infection with a monitored vaginal delivery was calculated (as an average weighted by sample sizes) from the results of three studies (Haverkamp et al., 1976, 1979; Gassner and Ledger, 1976) to be .037. The maternal expectation with a monitored vaginal delivery is thus a .037 chance of infection and a complementary .963 (= 1 - .037) chance of no infection and is a loss: ME_{VM} = (.037) (-.0001)+(.963) (0) = -.0000037. The estimated chance of maternal infection with an unmonitored vaginal delivery (similarly calculated) is .016, making ME_{VU} = -.0000016.

Similarly, the estimated chances of nonfatal maternal complications following cesarean delivery were calculated to be .422 with monitoring and .285 without. The figures are weighted averages derived from six studies: the three noted above, the studies by Gibbs and his associates (1976, 1978), and the one by Hagen (1975). The observed risk of maternal death of 3.1 per 10,000 cesarean deliveries is assumed to apply to both monitored and unmonitored cases. The maternal expectation with cesarean delivery after monitoring is a .422 chance of nonfatal complication, a .578 chance of an uncomplicated delivery, and a .00031 chance of death: ME_{CM} = (.422) (-.001) + (.578) (-.0002) + (.00031) (-300) = -.09354. In similar fashion, ME_{CU} is calculated to be -.09343.

We assume, in line with current national statistics, that 9.3 percent of unmonitored births have cesareans and that 12.5 percent of monitored births do. The change (expected loss) in maternal expectation due to having EFM is:

$$EL_M = (.032) (ME_{CM} - ME_{VU}) + (.093) (ME_{CM} - ME_{CU})$$
$$+ (.875) (ME_{VM} - ME_{VU})$$
$$= -.0030 + (-.0000102) + (-.0000018)$$
$$= -.0030.$$

The first term corresponds to cesareans caused by EFM; the second to somewhat worse outcomes with EFM among mothers who would have had cesareans in any case; and the third to somewhat worse outcomes with EFM and vaginal delivery.

The expectation due to neonatal infections is also a loss: $EL_{NI} = (.005)(-.0001) = -.0000005$.

Weighing Benefits Against Risks. Summing these components, we find that the gains sum to .0031 and the losses to .0030. This indicates that there is a slight advantage on expectation to monitoring in the average birth. Remembering that our units are the value of averting one case of severe mental retardation, we can interpret the net advantage of EFM as equal to the value of having a .001 chance of averting severe mental retardation per birth monitored. Only three terms make much difference in calculating the net advantage of EFM: The gains in terms of likely perinatal mortality reduction (value = .0021) and of likely reduction in severe mental retardation (value = .0010) marginally outweigh the likely loss due to maternal mortality caused by EFM (value = −.0030). The other factors, maternal and neonatal infections, are relatively insignificant.

Importance of Components of Uncertainty. The importance of uncertainty regarding the various parameters shown in Table 6.4 can now be calculated. For each parameter, we calculate the difference between the net expected worth of EFM assuming the high and the low values of the parameter. That is, taking the reduction in perinatal mortality to be zero (its lower bound), the net expected outcome with fetal monitoring would be a loss of .0020. If perinatal mortality would decrease by 0.94 percent with EFM (its upper bound), the expected gain with EFM would be .0046. The difference is .0066, as shown in the table. Similar calculations are made for the other parameters, and the results are shown in the second column of the table. We can see there that the prospective value of EFM is affected most by uncertainty regarding the connection between EFM and the CSR: .0090 units. To put the importance of the other parameters into perspective, we divide all entries in the second column by .0090. The results are shown in the third column and essentially indicate the importance of uncertainty about the

TABLE 6.4 Absolute and Relative Importance of Uncertainty Concerning EFM Parameters as Calculated Using Clinical Decision Analysis

1. Parameter	2. Absolute Importance of the Uncertainty: Difference in Net Gain with EFM Figured with High and Low Bounds for the Parameter Estimates	3. Relative Importance of the Uncertainty: Importance of Parameter Uncertainty Compared with That of the CSR Increase	4. Numbers of Pages Devoted to Parameter in Section III of the Report of the Task Force on Predictors of Fetal Distress (NIH, 1979)
1. Reduction in perinatal morality	.0066	.73	14
2. Reduction in severe mental retardation	.0025	.28	11
3. Maternal infection rate with EFM and vaginal delivery	.0000032	.00036 ⎫	
4. Maternal infection rate with EFM and cesarean delivery	.000024	.0027 ⎬	4
5. Rate of scalp abscesses with EFM	.0000005	.00006	3
6. Increase in CSR with EFM	.0090	1.00	19

NOTE: Units for column 2 are proportions of the value of preventing a case of severe mental retardation. Figures in column 3 are obtained by dividing corresponding entries in column 2 by .0090.

125

individual parameters relative to the importance of uncertainty about the impact on the CSR. This column suggests that uncertainty about the reduction in perinatal mortality is roughly 73 percent as important as uncertainty about the CSR. Uncertainty about the reduction in severe mental retardation is 28 percent as important, while uncertainty about rates of maternal and neonatal infections is much less important. The fourth column shows the number of pages devoted to each issue in one section of the report by the Task Force on Predictors of Fetal Distress (National Institutes of Health, 1979). Comparison of the third and fourth columns shows that the higher the significance of the various elements of uncertainty as we have calculated it, the more attention was devoted to those elements in this report.

Benefit-Cost Analysis

Following Banta and Thacker (1979a), we calculate benefits and costs per 1,000 monitorings. The results are shown in Table 6.5. This indicates that costs outweigh benefits by roughly $12,000 per 1,000 births. We calculate the impact of parameter uncertainty on the net benefits of EFM in the same way as for the clinical decision analysis. We measure the difference between the net benefits estimated with the high and low values of the parameters. This is shown in Table 6.6. This table indicates that, from the economic point of view, uncertainty regarding reduction in perinatal mortality has greatest import, followed by uncertainty regarding increases in the CSR and reduction in mental retardation. At much lower levels of significance is uncertainty concerning maternal and neonatal infections. These latter items do, however, assume greater relative importance than in the framework of clinical decision analysis.

DISCUSSION

The clinical decision analysis has indicated that, on expectation, it is marginally better to monitor than not to do so. In

TABLE 6.5   Benefit-Cost Analysis of EFM for 1,000 Average Births

Benefits		
1. 2.95 perinatal lives saved at $33,370		$ 98,400
2. 1.0 case of severe mental retardation prevented at $57,997		$ 58,000
Total Benefits		$156,400
Costs		
1. Monitoring 1,000 births at $50		$ 50,000
2. 32 additional cesareans at $2,300		$ 73,600
3. 93 mothers with cesarean section with more infections due to EFM (.422 - .285) times $1,140		$ 14,500
4. 875 mothers with vaginal delivery but more infection (.037 - .016) times $570		$ 10,500
5. 32 additional mothers with cesarean section infection rates (.422) ($1,140) - (.016) ($570)		$ 15,100
6. .01 maternal deaths at $114,057		$ 1,100
7. 5 fetal scalp infections at $700		$ 3,500
Total Costs		$168,300
Net Costs		$ 11,900

benefit-cost analysis, the situation is reversed. These are not, however, the important lessons of the analyses. Based on present information, monitoring may truly be vastly better or vastly worse on expectation than not monitoring. The uncertainty about the possible net benefit or the possible net harm of monitoring far exceeds the current best estimates of any net advantage or net disadvantage for the technique. The magnitude of the prevailing uncertainty and the consequent need for further study are the main messages of the analyses performed.

Methodological Issues

Clinical decision analysis is a suitable decision logic when concern for health outcomes predominantly guides decision-

TABLE 6.6 Absolute and Relative Importance of Uncertainty Concerning EFM Parameters as Calculated Using Benefit Calculated Using Benefit-Cost Analysis

1. Parameter	2. Absolute Importance of Uncertainty: Difference in Net Benefits of EFM Figured with High and Low Bounds for the Parameter Estimates	3. Relative Importance of Uncertainty: Importance of Parameter Uncertainty Compared with That of Perinatal Mortality Reduction
1. Reduction in perinatal morality	$313,700	1.00
2. Reduction in severe mental retardation	$145,000	.46
3. Maternal infection rate with EFM-vaginal delivery	$ 21,100	.07
4. Maternal infection rate with EFM-cesarean delivery	$ 34,200	.11
5. Rate of scalp abscesses with EFM	$ 3,500	.01
6. Increase in CSR with EFM	$269,500	.86

NOTE: Units for column 2 are changes in expected net births per 1,000 monitorings. Figures in column 3 are obtained by dividing corresponding entries in column 2 by $313,700.

making. Benefit-cost analysis is more appropriate when economic considerations weigh heavily in decisions. Some cautionary words regarding both disciplines, as used here, are in order.

Values for Clinical Decision Analysis. The values used should not be taken for more than they are: only the median estimates of a nonrandom group of persons derived from a set of questions that were admittedly hard to conceptualize and to answer. The respondents were primarily physicians, whose values may differ significantly from those of the general population. Differences among respondents were large. As one example, judgments of the maximum risk of maternal death acceptable to prevent a case of severe mental retardation ranged from one in 35 to one in 2000 and to 2 respondents who would accept no risk whatever. Analysis of these value differences would be a fascinating study requiring more extensive interviewing than we did. We obtained the values shown in Table 6.3 not out of primary interest in them but to see what light they would shed on the various components of uncertainty regarding EFM.

Using the Best Probability Estimates. The slight expected advantages for monitoring found in clinical decision analysis and for not monitoring found in benefit-cost analysis derive from the choice of best probability estimates. Use of other probabilities could have led to different analytic findings: either quite favorable or unfavorable to monitoring. Another analyst might, for instance, give as the best estimate of the increase in cesarean rate due to EFM either 3 or 99 per 1000 deaths. Such estimates would not be necessarily wrong or inexpert or biased. Unprejudiced experts could reasonably arrive at and defend, any figure within this interval—indeed, the interval endpoints were chosen on precisely that criterion. Use of other probabilities (or other values) might lead to EFM being found far better or far worse than no monitoring. We are using clinical decision analysis not so much to discover whether EFM is or is not net-beneficial as: (1) to show that the prevailing range of uncertainty can dramatically affect the attractiveness of monitoring, and (2) to determine the relative importance of the various components of uncertainty.

Issues Neglected

Considerations of space have limited our discussion to the main sources of uncertainty concerning fetal monitoring. In so doing, we have not addressed several issues of concern. Such issues include:

(1) The variation among personal values. Our clinical decision analysis depended on personal valuation of obstetric outcomes. These values vary considerably across different persons—a phenomenon meriting much more study than was possible here. Although this variability should influence individual decisions, it should not affect the main conclusions of this chapter.

(2) The variability of other parameters. We have taken from the literature such parameters as the rate of maternal death following cesarean section and the costs of various complications. These parameters are also subject to uncertainty which could be analyzed using the methodology presented in this chapter.

(3) Subsequent cesareans. In the United States, it is a common practice to deliver by cesarean section all mothers with previous cesarean delivery. We have not included in our analyses the implications of sectioning for subsequent births. This would have required estimating several parameters on which data are sparse, and would have led to results less favorable for monitoring. Our analyses could thus be interpreted as being most pertinent for mothers not planning to have more children.

(4) Specific confounders in interpreting studies. Controversy has surrounded the principal studies of EFM. Some RCTs (Haverkamp et al., 1976; Renou et al., 1976) have had apparent bad-luck randomization—statistically significant differences between the monitored and unmonitored groups. In some studies (Haverkamp et al., 1976, 1979), auscultation of the unmonitored group by trained personnel was more intensive than usual. This suggests that such auscultation might have improved outcomes while simultaneously obscuring the effects of monitoring. If so, more intensive auscultation would represent a reasonable alternative both to EFM and to usual procedure without EFM.

(5) Level of risk. We have, due to data limitations, been considering the monitoring of the average birth. In reality, there is a broad

variety of situations to be considered. Some—in general, the labors at higher risk—will be prospectively much more beneficial to monitor than others. Ideally, different analyses would determine the appropriateness of EFM for different situations. Without data broken down by patient characteristics, this is impossible.

Impact on Clinical Decision-Making

Given the closeness of the prospective benefits and costs of EFM and the magnitude of uncertainty, it would be presumptuous to say that harm is being done either by those who monitor or by those who do not. In examining the effects of obstetrician beliefs, we must look at other results, or possible results.

Overall Certainty. Obstetricians, on the basis of current evidence, are more certain than they should be. Those favoring EFM tend to exaggerate its benefits and to minimize its costs. EFM opponents do the opposite. For some patients, this may be well: It may be less anxiety-provoking to have an obstetrician who strongly holds some technically unwarranted opinion about EFM than an obstetrician who admits that we really do not know now whether EFM is net-beneficial. On the other hand, admission of uncertainty by obstetricians may lead to more truly informed consent by the patient.

Perinatal Mortality. It was seen that the obstetricians tended to give estimates of perinatal mortality reduction via EFM that conformed closely to the literature.

Brain Damage. Obstetrician estimates of severe mental retardation saved by EFM paralleled those found in the literature. Their estimates of mild mental retardation averted via monitoring were more optimistic than study findings. This seems to spring from a belief in a strong linkage between hypoxia and mild mental retardation, when, in fact, most hypoxic neonates develop normally.

Maternal Infections. Obstetrician estimates of maternal infections due to EFM were lower than those in the literature. This seems to reflect obstetricians' focus on the increased infection rate among vaginally delivered mothers, which is proportionately more noticeable. More important is the increase among mothers delivered by cesarean. This is, however, less evident because of the generally high rates of infection among these mothers. The low estimates might also derive from exceptionally low rates of infection at the obstetricians' own hospitals. The underestimates, in any case, do not matter greatly: Maternal infection rates are much less important than other factors in determining the appropriateness of monitoring.

Neonatal Infections. The median estimate of neonatal infections seems low. As with maternal infections, this underestimate may reflect the experience of individual hospitals, but it is not important relative to other decision factors.

Increased Cesarean Sectioning. Most obstetricians in our sample seemed to believe that EFM causes negligible increase in the cesarean section rate. Several individuals, in fact, felt certain that the judicious combination of EFM and fetal scalp sampling actually reduces the CSR. These perceptions, for the most part, were based on personal or institutional experience and on selective citation of the literature. Individuals who held the opposite view—that EFM substantially increases the CSR—were equally secure in their belief and comparably selective in their choice of references. Despite strong polarization of professional opinion, the obstetricians were unwilling to give numerical estimates of EFM effect on the CSR. This seems indicative of the tremendous prevailing uncertainty. Even so, the obstetricians would not admit that they were unsure of their stated positions.

Potential Danger. We have seen the present difficulty in demonstrating conclusive advantages either for or against using EFM. Because of this, no substantial cost can be definitively associated with any of the possible obstetrician misperceptions concerning EFM risks and benefits discussed here. However, a potential danger lurks: If subsequent research demonstrated significant advantages for using or for not using EFM, obstetricians might be unwilling to renounce their previous, strongly held opinions and to alter their use of EFM. On the other hand, their apparent excessive certainty now might simply be a professional pose which can be easily modified or even abandoned if and when convincing contrary evidence comes to light.

Impact on Acquisition and Utilization Decisions

We have presented a benefit-cost analysis that might be used in guiding hospital acquisition of EFM equipment. In fact, such benefit-cost considerations play a small role in guiding or regulating the spread of EFM. Monitoring equipment is inexpensive relative to other medical devices, and is not subject to capital expenditure controls, such as Certificate of Need. In making the purchase decisions, hospitals are generally guided by perceived patient demand for services and by the expressed equipment needs of medical staff who often desire to be at the technological forefront of their respective specialties. Since the expenses of fetal monitoring can easily be billed to patients and third-party payers (Banta and Thacker, 1979b), no substantial economic factors constrain the acquisition and utilization of EFM equipment. In fact, evidence suggests that the sizable net revenue obtained from EFM use may serve as an inducement to equipment purchase (Cohen and Cohodes, 1980). If, however, research were to show conclusively that the clinical disadvantages of EFM outweigh the advantages (clinical as well as financial), equipment dissemination would be slowed, if not arrested completely. But so long as a substantial segment of the obstetric community continues to believe that EFM is net-beneficial, hospitals must acquire the equipment. To do otherwise would risk losing patients and young obstetricians.

Consequences for Evaluation Decisions

The most important conclusions of this study concern the evaluation decisions. We in the United States are currently spending hundreds of millions of dollars annually on EFM (Banta and Thacker [1979a] estimate over $400 million) without knowing whether its advantages exceed its disadvantages. If net-disbeneficial, this money is being wasted; if net-beneficial, currently unmonitored births should be monitored. The prospective gains in understanding better the effects of EFM overshadow the costs of requisite evaluations which, in turn, dwarf actual, current spending on evaluation of EFM. Our analysis indicates the following:

(1) Substantial evaluative emphasis should fall on perinatal mortality, brain damage, and cesarean sectioning. In comparison to these factors, the potential worth of better knowledge about maternal and neonatal infections is trifling.

(2) Attention should be given to differentiating births by risk factors. Currently, it seems that EFM is more desirable for high-risk than for low-risk births. It is important to know what identifiable risk factors argue for EFM and what are appropriate cutoff points for its use.

(3) More attention should be given to improving methods of interpreting monitor information and of deciding on cesarean sectioning. Obstetricians vary greatly in their operant definitions of fetal distress, in their interpretations of specific fetal heart rate patterns, and in the nature and timing of their decisions to take corrective actions (Cohen, 1980). Evaluative emphasis should be placed on the predictive value of specific monitor patterns and on the appropriateness of indicated actions—fetal scalp sampling and cesarean delivery.

(4) More attention should be given to values. Obstetricians disagree among themselves and with patients over the values of different obstetrical outcomes. Patient values depend on subjective taste and

stage of life. Attitudes toward mild and severe mental retardation, perinatal death, and maternal death have tremendous impact on the advisability of monitoring and of performing cesareans given certain indications. Patient and obstetrical attitudes are, however, rarely thought through, and patient attitudes are often poorly communicated to obstetricians. Consequently, the idiosyncratic values of individual obstetricians generally govern clinical decisions.

The attitudes of obstetricians toward evaluation of EFM are varied. Some call for further, large-scale RCTs. Others feel, however, that the net advantages of EFM are so great that it would be unethical to permit their patients to participate in randomized trials. A substantial minority feels that the government, in particular, should not meddle in the evaluation of EFM.

Consequences for Developmental Decisions

There is little consensus among obstetricians about the future of their technology. This lack of knowledge and certainty among practicing obstetricians about future technological trends is not of great consequence; it will not hamper research and development. These activities depend instead on the innovativeness of the electronics industry in consultation with a small number of obstetricians.

Our study does duggest that attention should be paid to two aspects of technological development:

(1) The importance of specific indicators of fetal distress. Both clinical decision analysis and benefit-cost analysis indicate that the main danger of EFM is that it may lead to unnecessary cesareans. This argues for developing diagnostically specific technologies: those that will avoid unnecessary cesareans. To some extent, continuous

tissue pH measurement is such a technology. However, the incentives of both technology developers and of obstetricians may not place a sufficient premium on the specificity of diagnosis. This could argue for a limited governmental role in promoting the development of more specific EFM devices.

(2) The difficulty of evaluating amid rapid technological change. It is possible that EFM, as currently practiced, is on balance clinically harmful and that the hundreds of millions of dollars spent on it are worse than wasted. Some studies indicating this have emerged and have been met with the argument that EFM use is continuously improving—that obstetricians are gaining skill in using it and that increased use of fetal scalp blood sampling is strengthening standard practice. No evaluation, in this light, is worth doing or heeding since, in examining yesterday's technology, it could not speak to the use of today's. One possible solution is to limit the introduction of new technologies into clinical practice until their net desirability has been evaluated. The Task Force on Predictors of Fetal Distress (National Institutes of Health, 1979) has endorsed this principle.

CONCLUSIONS

We conclude that there is substantial uncertainty about the benefits, costs, and risks of electronic fetal monitoring. Reducing this uncertainty is the role of evaluation and could lead to dramatic changes in decisions on acquiring and using EFM equipment. Obstetricians seem to have dismissed this uncertainty prematurely, perhaps because it reassures their patients or because it is so conceptually and psychologically troublesome. Uncertainty is, after all, difficult and often unpleasant to think about. Most obstetricians, in any event, have convinced themselves that EFM is either clearly good or clearly bad. In clinical decisions as well as in purchase decisions, there is potential, though not clearly demonstrable, harm in this attitude; the current prevailing uncertainty is so large that determinations to use or not to use, or to buy or not to buy, EFM equipment cannot be proven wrong or be severely criticized. The principal danger arises when an attitude of unwarranted certainty is carried over to evaluation decisions. This leads to studies and to sample sizes insufficient to dispel materially the uncertainty—even though the potential gain of larger studies is great. Evaluative decision makers may often share the obstetricians' reluctance to confront uncertainty. They would do well to overcome this reluctance and to focus on uncertainty—how large it is, what its components are, what its consequences are, and what aspects should have evaluative priority.

NOTES

1. Cost-effectiveness analysis is commonly used in such decisions, yet is difficult to apply here due to the disparity of outcomes: Perinatal deaths must be made commensurate with maternal deaths, infections, cesarean sectioning, and mental retardation. Even the use of quality-adjusted life years is here questionable, due to the difficult comparability of maternal and neonatal years and of mentally retarded and healthy states. We decided accordingly to adopt benefit-cost analysis in preference to cost-effectiveness analysis.

2. We might have diverged from Banta and Thacker by assuming a lower discount rate, as favored by many analysts. This would have made fetal lives still more valuable in comparison to maternal lives—a valuation that, especially in the light of the findings in clinical decision analysis, would have seemed a wild misstatement of actual, operant values.

3. If forced to quantify the uncertainty associated with these limits, we would estimate a .1 chance that the true figure is less than the lower limit and the same chance that it exceeds the upper limit. The possibility is thus left open that EFM may actually increase perintal mortality and, in the next section, brain damage.

REFERENCES

AMATO, J. C. (1977) "Fetal monitoring in a community hospital: a statistical analysis." Obstetrics and Gynecology 50: 269-274.

BANTA, H. D. and S. B. THACKER (1979a) "Costs and benefits of electronic fetal monitoring: a review of the literature." DHEW Publication (PHS) 79-3245. Washington, DC: Government Printing Office.

––– (1979b) "Policies toward medical technology: the case of electronic fetal monitoring." American Journal of Public Health 69: 931-935.

BIRCH, H. G., S. A. RICHARDSON, D. BAIRD SIR et al. (1970) Mental Subnormality in the Community: A Clinical and Epidemiological Study. Baltimore: William & Wilkins.

CHAN, W. H., R. H. PAUL, and J. TOEWS (1973) "Intrapartum fetal monitoring–maternal and fetal morbidity and perinatal mortality." Obstetrics and Gynecology 41: 7-13.

COHEN, A. B. (1980) Doctoral dissertation in progress, Harvard University.

––– and D. R. COHODES (1980) "Certificate of need and low capital cost technology: the case of electronic fetal monitoring." Urban Systems Research and Engineering, Inc., report to the Bureau of Health Planning, HRA, DHEW.

CONLEY, R. and A. MILUNSKY (1975) "The economics of prenatal genetic diagnosis," in A. Milunsky (ed.) The Prevention of Genetic Disease and Mental Retardation. Philadelphia: W. B. Saunders.

DILTS, P. V. (1976) "Current practices in antepartum and intrapartum fetal monitoring." American Journal of Obstetrics and Gynecology 126: 491-494.

EDINGTON, P. T., J. SIBANDA, and R. W. BEARD (1975) "Influence on clinical practice of routine intra-partum fetal monitoring." British Medical Journal 3: 341-343.

EVRARD, J. R. and E. M. GOLD (1977) "Cesarean section and maternal mortality in Rhode Island." Obstetrics and Gynecology 50: 594-597.

FEDER, H. M., E. C. MacLEAN, and R. MOXON (1976) "Scalp abscess secondary to fetal scalp electrode." Journal of Pediatrics 89: 808-809.

GASSNER, C. B. and W. J. LEDGER (1976) "The relationship of hospital-acquired maternal infection to invasive intrapartum monitoring techniques." American Journal of Obstetrics and Gynecology 126: 33-37.

GIBBS, R. S., P. M. JONES, and C.G.Y. WILDER (1978) "Internal fetal monitoring and maternal infection following cesarean section: a prospective study." Obstetrics and Gynecology 52: 193-197.

GIBBS, R. S., H. M. LISTWA, and J. A. READ (1976) "The effect of internal fetal monitoring on maternal infection following cesarean section." Obstetrics and Gynecology 48: 653-658.

HAGEN, D. (1975) "Maternal febrile morbidity associated with fetal monitoring and cesarean section." Obstetrics and Gynecology 46: 260-262.

HAMILTON, L. A., W. GOTTSHALK, D. VIDYASAGER et al. (1978) "Effects of monitoring high-risk pregnancies and intrapartum FHR monitoring in perinates." International Journal of Gynecology and Obstetrics 15: 483-490.

HAVERKAMP, A. D., M. ORLEANS, S. LANGENDOERFER et al. (1979) "A controlled trial of the differential effects of intrapartum fetal monitoring." American Journal of Obstetrics and Gynecology 134: 399-412.

HAVERKAMP, A. D., H. E. THOMPSON, J. G. McFEE, and C. CETRULO (1976) "The evaluation of continuous fetal heart rate monitoring in high-risk pregnancy." American Journal of Obstetrics and Gynecology 125, 3: 310-320.

HOBBINS, J. C., R. FREEMAN, and J. T. QUEENAN (1979) "The fetal monitoring debate." Obstetrics and Gynecology 54: 103-109.

HON, E. H. (1960) "Apparatus for continuous monitoring of the fetal heart rate." Yale Journal of Biology and Medicine 32: 397-399.

KELLY, V. C. and D. KULKARNI (1973) "Experiences with fetal monitoring in a community hospital." Obstetrics and Gynecology 41: 818-824.

KELSO, I. M., R. J. PARSONS, G. F. LAWRENCE, S. S. ARORA, D. K. EDMONDS, and I. D. COOKE (1978) "An assessment of continuous fetal heart rate monitoring in labor: a randomized trial." American Journal of Obstetrics and Gynecology 131, 5: 526-532.

LEE, W. K. and M. S. BAGGISH (1976) "The effect of unselected intrapartum fetal monitoring." Obstetrics and Gynecology 47: 516-520.

LOW, J. A., R. S. GALBRAITH, D. MUIR et al. (1978) "Intrapartum fetal asphyxia: a preliminary report in regard to long-term morbidity." American Journal of Obstetrics and Gynecology 120: 525-533.

National Institutes of Health (1979) "Predictors of intrapartum fetal distress," Part III of Antenatal Diagnosis, NIH Publication 79-1973. Washington, DC: Author.

——— (1978) "The biomedical research community: its place in consensus development." Journal of the American Medical Assocation 239: 5-9.

NEUTRA, R. R., S. E. FIENBERG, S. GREENLAND, and E. A. FRIEDMAN (1978) "Effect of fetal monitoring on neonatal death rates." New England Journal of Medicine 299: 324-326.

Obstetrical Practices in the United States (1978) Hearing before the Subcommittee on Health and Scientific Research, 95th Congress, 2nd Session, Senate Committee on Human Resources, April 17.

OKADA, D. M., A. W. CHOW, and V. T. BRUCE (1977) "Neonatal scalp abscess and fetal monitoring: factors associated with infection." American Journal of Obstetrics and Gynecology 129: 185-189.

PARER, J. T. (1978) "Benefits and detriments of fetal heart rate monitoring." Seminars in Perinatology 2, 2: 113-118.

PAUL, R. H. and E. H. HON (1973) "Clinical fetal monitoring IV: experiences with a spiral electrode." Obstetrics and Gynecology 41: 777-780.

PLAVIDAL, F. J. and A. WERCH (1976) "Fetal scalp abscess secondary to intrauterine monitoring." American Journal of Obstetrics and Gynecology 125: 65-70.

QUILLIGAN, E. J. and R. H. PAUL (1975) "Fetal monitoring: is it worth it?" Obstetrics and Gynecology 45: 96-100.

RENOU, P., A. CHANG, I. ANDERSON, and C. WOOD (1976) "Controlled trial of fetal intensive care." American Journal of Obstetrics and Gynecology 126, 4: 470-476.

SHENKER, L., R. C. POST, and J. S. SEILER (1975) "Routine electronic monitoring of fetal heart rate and uterine activity during labor." Obstetrics and Gynecology 46: 185-189.

TUTERA, G. and P. L. NEWMAN (1975) "Fetal monitoring: its effect on the perinatal mortality and cesarean section rates and its complications." American Journal of Obstetrics and Gynecology 122: 750-754.

WEINRAUB, Z., E. CASPI, I. BROOK et al. (1978) "Perinatal outcome in monitored and unmonitored high-risk deliveries." Israel Journal of Sciences 14: 249-255.

WEINSTEIN, M. C. and H. FINEBERG (forthcoming) Clinical Decision Analysis. Philadelphia: W. B. Saunders.

WIECHETEK, W. J., T. HORIGUCHI, and T. F. DILLON (1974) "Puerperal morbidity and internal fetal monitoring." American Journal of Obstetrics and Gynecology 119: 230-232.

ABOUT THE AUTHORS

Alan B. Cohen is a doctoral candidate in health services administration at the Harvard School of Public Health. His doctoral research involved the application of clinical decision analysis in evaluating strategies for utilizing electronic fetal monitoring. He previously directed or participated in a number of evaluation studies involving federal and state health programs. His primary research interests include medical technology assessment, evaluation of health care practices and service delivery programs, and policy analysis for health planning and regulation. He is the principal author of a recent Bureau of Health Planning report on certificate of need and low capital cost technology.

Linda V. Esrov is a health services researcher in the Division of Intramural Research in the National Center for Health Services Research. She received her Ph.D. in psychology from Northwestern University and completed a two-year post-doctoral fellowship in evaluation and research methodology. Her major research interest is the evaluation of health intervention, and she has published and presented papers concerning general evaluation methodology, the evaluation of emergency medical services systems, and patients' evaluations of hospital care.

John P. Goetz received his B.A. from Wheaton College, Wheaton, Illinois, with majors in mathematics and economics. His mathematical and computer skills were invaluable in the preparation of this manuscript. He presently is working toward a Master of Business Administration at the Northwestern University Graduate School of Business.

Olga M. Haring holds the rank of professor in the Departments of Medicine and of Community Health and Preventive Medicine at the Northwestern University Medical School, Chicago. She has designed the Northwestern University Computerized Medical Record Summary System, which provides not only a summary of the medical record, but also recommendations concerning the care of patients. She has been continuously engaged in research as Principal Investigator since 1956 in projects funded by the Public Health Service or Chicago Heart Association, and has actively been engaged in teaching medical students and directing research studies of medical students from the Evanston campus since 1965. She is a board certified and recertified internist and cardiologist.

James L. Rogers is Assistant Professor in the Department of Psychology at Wheaton College, Wheaton, Illinois, and a research associate in the Department of Medicine, Northwestern University Medical School, Chicago. For the past several years he has conducted evaluation research in the area of man-machine performance in medicine, and he is presently the Principal Investigator of a study entitled "Automated Record Summaries: Analysis of an Experiment." He has published evaluation studies in the field of computerized electrocardiographic interpretation and automated medical information technology. He is actively involved in research in the treatment of schizophrenia.

Lee Sechrest is Director of the Center for Research on Utilization of Scientific Knowledge at the Institute for Social Research, and Professor in the Department of Medical Care Organization at the School of Public Health, both at the University of Michigan. Previously he was Professor of Psychology at Florida State University, where he taught courses in research methodology and program evaluation. Prior to that he was at Northwestern University, where he was involved in the development of the university's training program in evaluation research. He has written nearly one hundred articles and is coauthor of six books, the best known of which is *Unobtrusive Measures.* He is on the editorial boards of a number of journals, including *Journal of Community Health, Journal of Abnormal Psychology,* and *Health Policy Quarterly.* He is chairman of the Panel of Editors for the *Journal Supplements Abstract Service,* and a consultant to a number of government and private agencies involved in development and evaluation of social interactions.

Mark S. Thompson is Assistant Professor of Health Services and Research Associate in the Center for the Analysis of Health Practices at the Harvard School of Public Health. His research has focused on applying decision analytic, economic, and evaluative techniques to policy analysis. He has written *Evaluation for Decision in Health Programmes* and *Benefit-Cost Analysis for Program Evaluation.*

Paul M. Wortman is Associate Professor in the Department of Medical Care Organization, School of Public Health, and Program Director in the Center for Research on Utilization of Scientific Knowledge at the Institute for Social Research at the University of Michigan. He was formerly Director of Northwestern University's Center for Evaluation Research and Co-director of the Division of Methodology and Evaluation Research in the Department of Psychology. He is interested in the evaluation of medical technology and the development and application of new analytic methods through secondary analysis of health and educational data and enhancing the policy relevance of evaluation research.

William H. Yeaton is a Research Investigator in the Center for Research on Utilization of Scientific Knowledge at the Institute for Social Research of the University of Michigan. He obtained his Ph.D. in school psychology at Florida State University. His research interests include behavioral community psychology, empirical validation of procedures for diffusion of effective treatment, estimation of magnitudes of experimental effects, comparison of visual and statistical analyses of data, and program evaluation. He received his B.A. from the University of New Hampshire.